ALSO BY GINA CAMPBELL

Panning for Your Client's Gold:
12 Lean Clean Language Processes

Mining Your Client's Metaphors:
A How-To Workbook on Clean Language and Symbolic Modeling
Basics Part One: Facilitating Clarity

Mining Your Client's Metaphors:
A How-To Workbook on Clean Language and Symbolic Modeling
Basics Part Two: Facilitating Change

Hope

IN A CORNER OF MY

Heart

A HEALING JOURNEY
THROUGH THE
DREAM-LOGICAL WORLD
OF INNER METAPHORS

GINA CAMPBELL

BALBOA.PRESS

A DIVISION OF HAY HOUSE

Balboa Press books may be ordered through booksellers or by contacting:

Balboa Press
A Division of Hay House
1663 Liberty Drive
Bloomington, IN 47403
www.balboapress.com
844-682-1282

Print information available on the last page.

ISBN: 979-8-7652-2789-3 (sc)
ISBN: 979-8-7652-3496-9 (hc)
ISBN: 979-8-7652-2790-9 (e)

Balboa Press rev. date: 09/26/2022

TABLE OF CONTENTS

Introduction

Discovering what you don't know you know can change everything.

What if you were to find out that you can have a calm sea to surround your heart and gently lull it with lapping waves when it gets agitated? What if there was a fountain in your gut that sprays the Water of Life, connecting you always with the energy of Source? Wouldn't it be wonderful if there was a switch just behind your right ear that you could flip to keep the knowing of your head, heart, and gut flowing, so that all three would contribute to your decision making?

Hidden below your conscious awareness are metaphors like these, metaphors that influence how you experience the world and handle what life brings. Your feelings, your thoughts, your actions, your responses to what happens each day are influenced by these metaphors. And you created them. Unconsciously, when you encountered something challenging in the past, you selected a metaphor that captured what the experience was like. Based on the logic of how these symbols function (how waves lap, fountains spray, and switches turn things on and off), you filed away some lessons as to how to respond the next time you face some similar situation.

It doesn't matter if you are aware of your internal metaphors or not. They silently direct what you do. They determine the patterns your mind/body system follows.

And this can be a good thing. If you chose an appropriate metaphor based on an accurate reading of the situation and came up with a successful strategy to handle it, the metaphor would support you well. A calming sea or a handy switch could be just the ticket.

But sometimes the metaphors you chose to guide your reactions and choices were based on a misunderstanding or incomplete information. Perhaps you were young and what seemed like a good solution for coping has turned out not to be so good after all. For example, you may have had to "hide inside a suit of armor" at one time in your life. But your circumstances are different now, and you no longer do. Yet here you are, subconsciously closing yourself off from the people around you. It may be time to update your metaphor by taking off the armor.

You may not know about your internal metaphors, but what you will discover in this book is that you can get to know them. And once you do, you can change them if they need to be changed. You can create new metaphors to refashion the mistaken ones and further strengthen or improve the helpful ones. These new metaphors will become the ones that guide you going forward. They will be the ones influencing your thoughts, feelings, and actions.

If you change your metaphors, you can transform your self.

As a counselor and life coach, I help people discover and explore their metaphors. The questions I ask and the strategies I use to determine what to direct clients to find out more about are from a counseling and coaching process called Clean Language. The method was first developed by counseling psychologist David Grove in the 1980s as he explored ways to work with trauma survivors. He questioned the standard treatments of the time that often re-traumatized clients by asking them to revisit the very events that had undone them in the first place. He wondered, is there a gentler and more effective way to help people heal? Ultimately, he concluded that the key to change lies in internalized metaphors.

David Grove upended much of what I learned in my graduate school counseling program and challenged me to ask some fundamental questions, ones that no professor ever encouraged me to ask. How do people establish their patterns? What needs to happen for people to change? Do people have experience and wisdom hidden within themselves that can foster shifts and solutions that endure? How can people access this inner wisdom? What might it look and sound like?

As I experienced Clean Language sessions for myself and as I used it to facilitate others' explorations, I came to fully appreciate that Grove was on to something important: our metaphors are not just helpful communication or artistic expressions. They play a much more fundamental and indispensable role.

Clean Language questions enable our conscious and subconscious parts to communicate with each other in their mutual language—metaphor. The parts can then use their combined wisdom to get greater clarity about who we are, what we deeply want and need, and how to get our mind/body systems in balance.

While a Clean Language session cannot rewrite our histories or change any reality over which we have no control, our internal metaphors can make a profound difference to our sense of well-being, resiliency, and wholeness. With the right internalized metaphors, we can meet the challenges of our lives with greater confidence and ease because the metaphors affect the way we interpret and respond to our experiences. They can help us adapt our strategies for living with the past, for managing in the moment, and for determining our futures to best support happy, healthy, and meaningful lives.

Now, fifteen years after first discovering Clean Language, I can say confidently that Grove's unique way of working with internal metaphors has made a profound difference for my clients. They are able to self-explore deeply enough to discover what they didn't know they knew. Clients often remark how, even in a first session, they feel they "get to the core" of their issues in a way no other approach has ever been able to reach. Often, they say something along the lines of, "I can't really put it into words, but something has shifted. I'm different. I'm different with other people. Somehow things are easier now." They are wowed by the richness, complexity, and wisdom of their inner worlds. They are completely convinced, as am I: their metaphors matter.

Julia's Sessions

If you are curious about the possibility of deep change, this book gives you a front-row seat as Julia discovers her internalized metaphors and what needs to change for her mind/body system to regain its equilibrium. I had twelve counseling sessions with her over the course of a year and a half. Julia is not her real name, and the names of her family members, her profession, and the details of her family members' lives have all been tweaked to protect her privacy. But all of Julia's words in the sessions are her own.

Like a narrator in a series of short stories, Julia takes us along as she takes a step forward in one session, a step back in the next, or to the side to some other mysterious place. Where is she going? Guided by some intuitive knowing, she is taking care of all the parts of her inner self as it rebalances after a huge shock sent her reeling. Her stories offer a window into a world of metaphors like the ones we all have below our conscious awareness. I suspect it is quite unlike what you might expect.

How to Read This Book

When you first start reading Clean Language questions on a static page, they may sound overly simplistic, repetitive, and grammatically awkward at times. The simplicity, the repetitions, and the unusual syntax are deliberate. Clean Language questions are not meant to be conversational so as not to draw the client into the give and take of a normal conversation with the facilitator.

A Clean Language session is an opportunity to explore yourself rather than have to explain yourself to another person. The questions are designed to help you get into a deeply mindful, inner-focused state. They require very little thought about what is being asked so your attention can be on the content being asked about. When you are on the receiving end of a Clean Language session, the questions do not sound odd, and the repetitions of what you have said do not seem boring or strange. Hearing your own words again is remarkably affirming and intriguing at the same time.

I encourage you to read this book slowly. Imagine hearing Julia speak her words. Imagine hearing me repeat them in a voice that matches her emphasis. My lines in the transcript are broken up, like a poem, to give you a sense of how I separate the phrases with plenty of pauses between them to allow Julia time to absorb the words she hears back. The repetitions and the pauses are as important as the questions themselves. They allow Julia to be more attentive to the words, images, and feelings she may have overlooked otherwise.

Between my questions and Julia's replies, I include brief comments about Clean Language and what is guiding my choice of questions to give you some sense of the logic behind them. They may also give you some ideas for your self-exploration.

Discover Yourself with Clean Language

You may wonder if you could have experiences like Julia's. Do you, too, have hidden metaphors that support and possibly thwart you? Having facilitated hundreds and hundreds of Clean Language sessions, I am confident in saying that you do; we all do. And you will get a chance to discover some of your metaphors as we go along.

At the end of each chapter is a suggested activity. If you are seeking to know yourself at a deeper level, give the exercises a go.

You don't have to be particularly creative or artistic or good at visualization to experience the sorts of things Julia does in her sessions. When you ask yourself Clean Language questions, the answers you get do not feel like you are making them up as they might if you were doing some creative writing. Rather, it feels like you are discovering what is already there. You witness and experience events as they unfold, like in a dream, but you also have a conscious role to play: you tune into your mind and body to recognize what is happening. If you don't like what you find, you decide what you want to happen instead and make choices and changes to further those aims.

You will need blank paper and markers or some other sketching materials for these activities. For one activity you will need some Post-its. And you may want to have a journal to record and process what you discover about yourself.

Now, come sit in the facilitator's chair with me for these twelve sessions. You don't need to know exactly what is happening for Julia; just be curious about what will happen next and how all the pieces of her puzzle will eventually work themselves into a luminous, new whole. Let her self-exploration inspire you to do some of your own as well.

Chapter One
A Little Green Plant

As Julia arrives for her first session, I am immediately aware of the sense of quiet grace she radiates. An attractive woman in her mid-60s with almost-white hair and vivid blue eyes, she settles in the chair of her choice. Arranging her belongings around her, she launches into her story without hesitation.

She is married to Alex, who is fifteen years her senior. When they were younger, their age difference seemed insignificant. But now that he is aging and his health is failing, she finds her role as a caregiver commands most of her time.

"I still love Alex deeply," she sighs, "but I miss acutely the activities we used to share, like sailing and traveling. My life is quieter now, growing more narrow by the week."

Julia, too, has some health issues with her eyesight and arthritis, problems she anticipates are likely to worsen in the future and limit her as well.

She brightens a bit as she describes the three grandchildren she delights in and her daughter Laura, who lives out of state. And then there is her other daughter.

It has taken Julia a while to work up to sharing this part of her story. Eight months ago, her daughter Barbara was killed in a car accident. Julia talks about the shock of her loss, of the phone that rang with what sounded like an ordinary ring, of the message that abruptly rocked her world.

"Each morning when I first wake up, gradually coming to consciousness, it feels like a normal day, and then I remember: Barbara is dead. It's like I've just gotten the phone call, and I've just realized all over again that she's gone." Julia takes a tight breath. "It's like no time has passed, though it's been months. That's why I have come to see you."

I consider the other losses, in addition to Barbara, that Julia is grieving: her old relationship with her husband, her own decline in health, the favorite activities that have had to be given up. She most likely has other losses in her long life, too. A new significant loss has a way of reviving other losses.

But rather than getting mired in more details about what has happened in either the distant or recent past, I begin by focusing Julia's attention on developing a clear idea of what it is she wants now. Problems that get in the way of achieving these desires will reveal themselves, and that is how we'll know what is relevant to work on and in what order she needs and wants to address them.

For Julia to put into her own words what it is she wants and to say it aloud will put all of her—mind, body, and spirit—in touch with what she is seeking. It is a vision that can encourage and sustain her until, in her words, she flowers again.

Session #1   **July 10th**

We pick up this Clean Language session where it formally begins once Julia has shared her background story. I ease in with a repetition of some of the exact words Julia has used to describe her family and her issues, letting her hear them again. They invite her to slip into a mindful, trance-like state where the outside world recedes and her focus can settle on her inner world.

"And Barbara, and she's gone.
And Alex and his declining health.
No more sailing and traveling.
And your health and limits.
And Laura and your grandchildren.
And when all that,
what would you like to have happen?"

Gazing out the window with a view of the garden, Julia begins. "I don't know. I have lost the sense of who I am and what I want."

She describes a life spent devoted to caring for others as the oldest of many siblings, as a wife and mother, and as a psychiatric nurse. Now she questions always having put others first.

"And lost a sense of who you are and what you want.
And caring for others... always having put others first.
And when all that,
what would you like to have happen now?"

"I want to leave the past behind and find a new source of motivation that comes up from my own sense of pleasure. I want a reason to get up in the morning, to go on."

"And a new source of motivation
that comes up from your own sense of pleasure.
And is there anything else about that sense of pleasure
that's your own?"

"I would know it."

"And you would know it.
And what kind of sense is that sense of pleasure
you would know?"

"It's a joyful, moving-forward feeling inside myself."

"And a joyful, moving-forward feeling inside.
And whereabouts inside?"

"In my heart."

"And in your heart.
And when there's a joyful, moving-forward feeling
inside you, in your heart,
then what happens?"

"My heart would be lighter." Julia pauses. She seems a bit surprised by this discovery. "I need to express myself truthfully, be who I am."

While speaking her truth and being who she is sound like fundamental needs, zeroing in on them too quickly and too directly is apt to put Julia "into her head," where she might start analyzing them. Getting her into that space creates the risk of leaving Julia's subconscious' stuck points unrevealed, especially as this is her first Clean Language session.

"And be who you are.
Express yourself truthfully.
And a lighter heart
and a joyful, moving-forward feeling.
And when a joyful, moving-forward feeling inside,
in your heart,
what kind of moving is that moving?"

"Oh, it's relaxed, natural, spontaneous, thoughtless. Not from my head."

"And when it's relaxed, natural, spontaneous, thoughtless,
a joyful, moving-forward,
that's a natural, joyful, moving-forward... like... what?"

"Like a newborn lamb, small, creamy white, and cute."

"And is there anything else about that small, creamy white, cute newborn lamb?"

"It's frolicking, just discovering how beautiful life is. She's free to have new experiences that develop as she sees beauty around her. She's full of energy, dumb, happy, less in her head. She's following her impulses."

Julia's eyes are closed, and she smiles weakly. "The lamb has lots more energy than I have. I don't feel I have any energy."

"And when you don't feel you have any energy,
what would you like to have happen?"

"I'd like to have that energy."

"And what kind of energy is that energy that lamb has,
that you'd like to have?"

"It's like a day in the park, happy children playing, a carousel, people to talk to. There's greenness out there. People are sailing on water."

"And whereabouts is that energy?"

"It's out there," Julia points to her right.

"And whereabouts out there?"

"Pretty far; I can't get to it." Julia pauses, shaking her head ever so slightly. "My sources have dried up. My DNA is completely dried up. I'm in the desert."

"And when energy is out there... (I gesture to Julia's right)
and happy children and people,
greenness and water,
and you're in a desert,
what would you like to have happen?"

"I want to water myself like a plant so it's thriving, not just surviving."

"And when you want to water yourself like a plant,
what kind of a plant is that plant?"

"A little green plant with long leaves."

For Julia, water not only helps her plant survive; it helps it thrive. Helping Julia get familiar with this helpful resource and any related symbols and locating them in and outside of herself in their metaphoric spaces will mean she will be able to find them again when she needs them.

"And when water a little green plant with long leaves,
where could that water come from?"

"It comes from the sky, from clouds that are far away. And they make things green."

"And is there anything else about those clouds,
far away,
that make things green?"

"I want to go to Greenness, but I can't get there from here. I'm too tired. And it can't come to me," she adds, sounding wistful. "I'd love to go to it."

"And when you'd love to go to Greenness,
what needs to happen so you can go there?"

"First, I need to pick up the plant."

"And can you pick up the plant?"

"Yes." Julia sounds confident. "Yes, I can."

"And as you pick up the plant,
is there anything else that needs to happen
for you to go to Greenness?"

"I need to walk out of the desert to go to the greener place. I need to put the plant down in a better location."

"And you need to pick up the plant,
and walk out of the desert,

and go to a greener place,
and put the plant down in a better location.
And is there anything else that needs to happen
for you to go to Greenness?"

"I need to keep the plant wet—keep it watered—to keep it alive until I can get to Greenness."

"And keep the plant wet, watered.
And is there anything else that needs to happen
until you can get to Greenness?"

"I don't think so."

"And when you pick up the plant and keep it wet,
and walk out of the desert,
and put it in a better location,
what kind of location is that better location?"

"There needs to be enough water there."

"And how much water is enough water to keep the plant wet
to keep it alive?"

"Just enough water."

"And just enough.
And where could just enough water come from?"

"I hope it rains so I can collect some."

"And when you hope it rains,
what kind of hope is that hope?"

"It's a creamy white, little light."

Creamy white, little. I am immediately reminded of the lamb in Julia's heart. But for now, I will just ask for more information and see what comes up. Perhaps the lamb will make a reappearance; perhaps the lamb metaphor has morphed into something else. Or it's possible they are not connected.

"And is there anything else about that creamy white, little light?"

"It's the size of a 50 cent piece, but with a jagged edge, like a piece of cloth."

"And when a creamy white, little light,
the size of a 50 cent piece,
with a jagged edge like a piece of cloth,
where is that little light?"

"In a corner of my heart." Julia sounds surprised. "I didn't know I had any hope, and here it is, in a small corner of my heart!"

"And a little light, there, in a small corner of your heart.
Hope!
And is there anything else that needs to happen
so you can have just enough water?"

"I need energy to start walking."

"And whereabouts could that energy to start walking come from?"

"The hope is what gives me the energy."

"And a little, creamy white light in a corner of your heart,
and energy to start walking.
And is there anything else that needs to happen
so you can have just enough water to keep that plant alive
until you get to Greenness?"

"I need a container to hold the water."

"And what kind of container is that container that could hold that water?"

"It's a small wooden bucket or bowl to catch the water."

"And where could that small wooden bucket or bowl come from?"

"It's outside of me." But then Julia questions her answer. "Maybe it's not outside me; maybe it's in myself."

Cupping her hands, Julia gestures as if she is moving water to the plant with slow, repetitive motions that last a full minute. We are both quiet for some time. "It's related to spending time alone, a period when I can care for myself, space just for me. I don't think anyone can give me the bucket but myself. I need to remember to hold it there. I have to be aware."

It's easy to skip over this last sentence, but I have found that "awareness" is often a distinctly separate step in people's inner processes that trips them up: they have to be aware, to notice that a step needs to be taken before they take it. A few more questions can reveal a hidden issue or a pattern that may have been undermining Julia's caring for herself, possibly for a very long time.

"And what kind of aware is that aware?"

"Aware of what I need."

"And what needs to happen
for you to be aware of what you need?"

"I need to give myself permission; it has to do with deserving."

"And permission.
And when you give yourself permission,
that has to do with deserving,
where could that permission come from?"

"It's located partly in my head and partly in my throat."

"And partly in your head,
and partly in your throat.
And when in your throat,
is there anything else about that permission,
there, in your throat?"

Julia squirms uncomfortably. "There's a choking feeling, anger. It's not appropriate for me to be the way I am. Something is stuck in my throat: words, self-expression. I feel like I'm holding back."

"And when choking feeling and anger,
and it's not appropriate to be the way you are,
and you're holding back,
what would you like to have happen?"

"I want to have the right to be. It's related to happiness, to the right to be." Julia shakes her head. "There's a strong, negative energy. There's a push down. There's a stuck."

I'm not clear whether the energy is being pushed down or it's doing the pushing.

"And what kind of push down is that push down?"

"It's both pushing down and trying to push up. It's definitely both! No wonder I have no energy! That's where my energy is going!"

"And no wonder you have no energy!
A pushing down and a trying to push up.
And when that's where your energy is going,
what would you like to have happen?"

"I need to focus more each day on finding something to do just because I want to do it. And know that's alright. I almost feel to do that makes me callous, like I don't care. I should just mourn and take care of my husband, but I'm exhausted."

And then Julia looks up, directly at me. We've been at it over an hour now. She looks tired, and her words and tone have shifted. She comes out of her immersion in her symbolic world, marveling at what she's discovered in the session and planning what she wants to do daily.

I invite Julia to draw a metaphor map, a picture of the metaphors that have come up in the session and where they are positioned on the paper in right relation to one another as she experienced them. Julia mentions again that she hadn't known hope was there, in her heart. She seems delighted and draws with evident pleasure.

As Julia draws, she retrieves another metaphor. "I've had an image of myself my whole life as an aircraft carrier. I am both the plane that is caught and the hook that grabs and holds the plane."

*   *   *   *   *

In the process of adding these details to her drawing, Julia continues to process and find connections to what she did in the session.

We didn't get to watering and moving the plant. We didn't finish addressing Julia's need for giving herself permission. Her last comments suggest she is still struggling with wanting to take care of others and take care of herself.

Some sessions seem to put right the dilemmas that arise; others end with more left to be done. Every session is but a segment of a larger whole that is the person's full experience of herself. We stop short of resolution, not knowing all that happened for Julia in this session, what it all means, and what needs to happen next.

Clean Language healing is not a linear process. Julia will revisit some metaphors as needed, and others will not appear again. Her inner wisdom will let her know what needs addressing and at what pace to move, as each session offers Julia an opportunity to learn more about herself.

Now it's your turn to discover something new about yourself.

Discover Yourself with Clean Language

Materials: a piece of blank paper and drawing materials, like markers or crayons. You may want a journal, too.

Because we are taught to be problem solvers, we tend to focus on problems. We know what we don't like, what we don't want. But what about what we want instead? Getting clarity on that can be helpful, sometimes profoundly so. I invite you to give this a try.

Think of a goal you have for yourself. It can be as cosmic as furthering your spiritual development or as specific and mundane as deciding what you would like for your birthday.

Avoid choosing something that depends on information from outside of you, such as, "I want to know more about Clean Language."

But you could say, "I want to be open to learning about new ways of exploring myself." This has a more personal focus; it's the sort of thing the Clean Language process is ideal for.

Since this is your first go at this, let me give you an example. By following the directions I'm going to give you in a moment, this is what might unfold in a typical session:

Starting Clean question and directive:

And what would you like to have happen or to know more about?

And draw a picture of what that would look like.

Once the drawing is complete, I offer the invitation:

And describe your picture.

Speaker: "I want to be open to learning about new ways of exploring myself. In my picture, I'm looking at a projection screen where I can see what there is to learn. There is light coming from my heart that radiates onto the screen with what it knows is my core truth. I have a magnifying glass to use, if I want to get into the nitty-gritty."

Here are some possible follow-up Clean Language questions I might ask:

And is there anything else about that screen?

And what kind of learn is that learn?

And is there anything else about that radiates?

And what kind of heart is a heart that radiates your core truth?

And is there anything else about that nitty-gritty?

Now, it's your turn. Write out the answer to this question:

And what would you like to have happen or to know more about?

Then do a simple sketch (stick figures or scribbles of color are fine; artistic talent doesn't matter in the least). Draw what your situation or state of being would look like if it was the way you would like it to be.

When you have finished the drawing, describe it aloud. You may want to jot down what you say. Then ask yourself these questions about any word or short phrase you say:

And is there anything else about that [fill in your word or phrase]*?*

And what kind of [fill in your word or phrase] *is that* [repeat same word or phrase]*?*

Just keep asking these same questions about a variety of words you say. If you discover anything new that belongs in your picture, add it. Then ask questions about that. Keep on going until you feel you have learned all there is to learn about what is in your drawing or until it feels right to stop. I suggest you give it at least ten minutes. What comes up in the first few minutes are generally things you already know; as you keep on exploring, what you don't know you know will begin to reveal itself.

If you like what you end up with, you may want to place your picture somewhere you can see it often to inspire you.

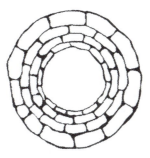

Chapter Two
Trapped Between Self and Black

Accessing your inner world of subconscious metaphors is actually pretty easy once you get good at noticing implied metaphors. They are metaphors that are subtly hinted at by words that suggest images—words like *push*, *percolate*, and *move forward*.

If you are curious about applying Clean Language to your own words, be on the lookout for Julia's implied metaphors as you read this chapter. Noticing hers will help you get better at noticing your own.

Session #2   **September 12ᵗʰ**

Julia is back from a long vacation. She is still grieving her daughter's death, she says, and still feels trapped by her aging husband's illness and needs. We begin as we did the first time: focusing on what Julia wants. Clean Language questions, with their slightly unusual wording and hypnotic repetition, invite the subconscious to speak up.

"And when still grieving your daughter's death,
and trapped by your aging husband's illness and needs,

what would you like to have happen?"

"I want to feel better and to move forward."

"And when feel better,
what kind of better is that better
you want to feel?"

"I'll have more energy to invest in other areas of my life, rather than in my past. Now the energy is taken up with sadness and grief, with the loss of Barbara and all that implies, and with all the losses for her, too."

"And is there anything else about that better
you want to feel?"

"I want to move ahead into the future better. I have a feeling it's going to be somehow, and in some ways, the same as I've always been, but there's a shift I need to make to put me in a better place. To let go of the past and move on. To invest in happier activities."

Julia drops her eyes to the floor. "But I'm not sure that's possible."

We are so often unaware of the metaphors implied in our choice of words. They simply roll off our tongues, hinting subtly at the way we have subconsciously structured our understanding of our world and ourselves. Which is why, with Clean Language, I repeat Julia's exact words back, slowing her down to notice more about them in a hypnotic way that reveals the deeper wisdom they contain. I begin with a word that she's used twice and that could be one of those implied metaphors.

"And more energy to invest in other areas of your life,
and invest in happier activities.
And when invest,
that's invest... like... what?"

"Like buying some stock in different companies I have."

"And what kind of stock is that stock
you want to invest in?"

"Long-term growth stocks. Like stocks (or perhaps she said stalks?) of flowers."

"And when flowers
and long-term growth,
is there anything else about that growth?"

"I could invest in flowers. They could flourish and bring me positive results."

"And what kind of flowers are those flowers
you could invest in?"

"They're thriving, blooming. They're positive, happy, beautiful, joyful!"

"And thriving, blooming flowers.
Positive, happy, beautiful, joyful!
And where are those thriving flowers?"

"I see an English country garden with anemones and poppies, yellow and orange. There's a beautiful mix of closely grown flowers of all colors. And there's laughter!"

"And an English country garden and flowers.
And laughter!
And when there's laughter,
where could that laughter come from?"

"Little children have come into the garden. It's a beautiful day. I'm investing in myself! I'm starting a company rather than buying one."

"And when investing in yourself,
and little children,
and a mix of flowers of all colors,
and an English country garden,
where is that garden?"

"I'm on the outside, looking at it."

"And when you're on the outside,

looking at it,
what would you like to have happen?"

"I'd like to be there! I'd like to have the little children with me, spending the afternoon, not doing anything special. Enjoying the day. Playing with the children. Looking at the flowers. Being in charge, running it. It makes me think of a nursery school, of my grandchildren in another state."

"And when a garden,
and being in charge
and running it,
is there anything else about that running it,
that being in charge?"

"It's growing something. I think of children, flowers, nursery schools, of joyful relationships. It has to do with my youth, with my husband, with an older frame of mind. Now I'm surrounded by endings rather than fresh starts."

Everyday reality intrudes into this idyllic scene. I acknowledge it, but rather than dwell on it, I redirect Julia back to what she wants instead.

"And when you're surrounded by endings
rather than fresh starts,
what would you like to have happen?"

"I want to see forward movement in my life! I'm surrounded by black, by caskets, by sickness."

Here is one of those moments when I sense a metaphor poised to reveal itself. The words "surrounded by endings" and "surrounded by black" catch my attention.

"And when you're surrounded by endings,
by sickness, by caskets, by black,
what's between you and black?"

"There's some space, not a whole lot. It's hard to breathe. It's a dank gray. It's not pleasant! I'm trapped in a place between self and black." Julia drops her head. "I feel like an old gray dishrag that needs to be thrown away. There's a sense the dishrag is worn out, used up." She picks up her head. "Part of me wants to break out."

"And some space,
and dank gray.
And part of you wants to break out.
And when break out,
that's break out... like... what?"

"It feels like I'm in a well. It's black and has a thick wall."

"And when you're in a well,
and it's black,
with a thick wall,
and part of you wants to break out,
what kind of break out is that break out?"

"I'd like to disappear and shoot up."

"And disappear and shoot up.
And when shoot up,
where would you like to shoot up to?"

"I see the sky. I see the sun." And Julia falls silent, her eyes moving under her closed lids. I sit quietly for a minute or more. Finally, she speaks again.

"I'm hovering over the well. I'm out." But Julia doesn't seem relived or pleased. I sense something more is going on, and I remain quiet as Julia's brow furrows, her eyes still closed. "It's all very nice, but part of me says I belong in the well."

"And part of you is out, hovering over the well.
And part of you says you belong in the well.
And when part of you is out
and part of you says you belong in the well,
that's... like... what?"

"There are two parts. I am being pulled very hard in two directions, being yanked by both arms."

I am reminded of the metaphor that Julia ended the last session with, the one of the plane on the aircraft carrier and the hook that pulls it—two tremendous opposing forces. Are these parts of herself being yanked related? Maybe. But right now she's in a well, and that's where we'll stay focused.

"And when you're being pulled in two directions
and both arms yanked,
what would you like to have happen?"

"I would like to be freed from the well, to have someone free me. I'm back in the well again. I don't want to be pushed out of the well. It's where I belong. It's the reality of the situation. I should try to fix the well. Lighten the darkness. Instead, I want to escape the whole thing!"

"And part of you wants to escape the whole thing!
And part of you says you belong in the well.
You should try to lighten the darkness.
And when you're pulled in two directions, arms yanked,
then what happens?"

"I'm looking for the light!"

"And where could that light come from?"

"Way up in the sky. There's a little reflection down here, on the wall of the well."

"And is there anything else about that little reflection,
there, on the wall of the well?"

"It's a couple of sunbeams, about one foot long. Sunbeams on the wall."

"And where on the wall are those sunbeams?"

"About midway up, a couple of feet over my head. They're still too high to reach."

"And when a couple of sunbeams are there,
a couple of feet over your head,

still too high to reach,
what would you like to have happen?"

"I have to find a ladder."

"And what needs to happen for you to find a ladder?"

"I have to look for it. I'm feeling around in the dark for something to stand on."

"And as you're feeling around,
then what happens?"

"It's dampness, coldness, moss on the slippery sides. There's a little water, and there's darkness. I want to get out of the well. If I can't do that, it would be nice to be able to touch the light, the warmth, the reflection, and to feel the sun on my hand."

"And you want to get out of the well
or touch the light, the warmth, the reflection,
feel the sun on your hand.
And is there anything else about that feel the sun on your hand?"

"It's a happy, cheery feeling of warmth, of joy, of life. It's a reflection of the positive. It wants to shine on me, to give me warmth, health, well-being, pleasure."

"And when Sun wants to shine on you
and wants to give you warmth,
health, well-being, pleasure.
And when you want to touch the light,
feel the Sun and the warmth on your hand,
then what happens?"

"It's shining on me now. I'm still in the well, but I feel its warmth, a sense of the loving sunbeam."

"And when you feel Sun now,
in the well,
and sense of the loving Sunbeam,
what happens to well?"

"The walls of the well go further out. The Sunbeam illuminates the area around me, and it is less gray now." Julia seems to relax ever so slightly, her shoulders easing. "The wall is still there, but I'm focused on the Sunbeam, on the sunshine. I'm enjoying the moment! Everything is golden.

"I'd like to be freed, but I don't want to be pushed out of the well. It's where I belong," she says. "It's the reality of the situation. I should try to stay there and fix it up. Lighten the darkness. Part of me wants to break out, but part of me doesn't have a need to break out. It's the part that wants to be there."

Oh, this is new! Julia had seemed so resigned when she said before that she belongs there. Now, she has discovered that part of her actually wants to be there.

"Part of me didn't have a need to break out. The wall is there, but there's also a future, a sense that there's something positive growing there."

"And when a sense something positive is growing,
is there a relationship between that growing in the well
and that English garden,
with anemones and yellow and orange poppies,
and children,
and blooming,
and laughter?"

"Yes! It's the same. It's something quite beautiful, and I want to be there. I am the flower! I want to be warmed, to be in the light, so I can flower."

"And you are the flower!
And when you're the flower,
what kind of flower are you?"

"The kind of flower that needs to open. An ordinary flower like a buttercup or a yellow cosmos."

"And can you open up?"

"I could, but I have to be the sun and the flower. It's easier to be the sun; it's harder to be the flower. I have to work out both."

"And what needs to happen for you to work out both, to be the sun and the flower?"

Julia opens her eyes and smiles. "I don't know. I'm going to try to keep the image of the sun and the flower and be both."

* * * * *

With a look that tells me she has left her symbolic metaphor world and returned to ordinary conscious awareness, we stop for now. I invite Julia to draw another metaphor map and to place it somewhere at home where she can see it between now and our next session to help her "keep the image."

Julia is taking the time she needs to address all the intricacies of her system to ready it for change. I recall her use of the phrase "long-term growth." Perhaps this is a suggestion that, on some level, she knows this healing is a long-term process. It is not to be rushed.

Discover Yourself with Clean Language

A key to getting to know your inner experience is to notice when your words could suggest a metaphor. Now, you don't want to be scrutinizing your every word for metaphors so diligently that you get all in your head and don't allow your experience to unfold. On the other hand, getting more attuned to the suggested/implied metaphors in your choice of words can be enlightening and great fun.

Some of your metaphors will be straightforward: a well, a flower, a ladder. Some are suggested more subtly and can be easily overlooked. They hint at what's just below that surface. Take this passage of Julia's:

"And more energy to invest in other areas of your life, and invest in happier activities. And when invest, that's invest... like... what?"

"Like buying some stock in different companies I have."

*"And what kind of stock is that stock
you want to invest in?"*

"Long-term growth stocks. Like stocks (or perhaps she said stalks?) of flowers."

*"And when flowers
and long-term growth,
is there anything else about that growth?"*

"I could invest in flowers. They could flourish and bring me positive results."

Julia is now ready to explore what she wants from the different perspective offered by thinking of growth as flowers. Continuing to ask questions about her exact words led to uncovering the wisdom her inner world can contribute, not just for this situation, but for other similar ones as well.

You, too, will be well-served by sticking to the Clean questions and your own exact words to allow your metaphors to emerge from your subconscious.

Examples: Here are some feelings and concepts that people often use metaphors to describe. Take your time asking yourself the questions; check in with your body and notice the images that come to mind. You can sketch out a picture of the metaphor or symbols. As you draw, you will likely discover more about them. And certainly, change any of these examples to suit yourself if they don't seem right. Once you get the hang of it, try coming up with some examples of your own.

*1. And when I push myself to [fill in the blank], that's push...
like... what?*

*2. And when I am focused on [fill in the blank], that's focused...
like... what?*

*3. And when I want to move forward with [fill in the blank], that's
move forward... like... what?*

4. And when I stand by what I say, that's stand by... like... what? And is there anything else about that stand by?

5. And when I feel upbeat about [fill in the blank], that's up... like... what?

6. And when I feel upbeat, what kind of beat is that beat?

Chapter Three
The Midwife of Flowers

In this next session, you will see again how the metaphors in Julia's inner world have wants and needs of their own. Some symbols cause problems and may have to be negotiated with. Other symbols prove to be resourceful allies that Julia wasn't aware she had.

Once a metaphor becomes personified, you may have noticed I start capitalizing its 'name' in the transcript. It reminds me to keep aware of its intentions and needs.

Session #3   **September 20th**

Julia reports that she had a sense of well-being that lasted for days after her last session. But she still hasn't let go of her grief for Barbara. She just can't.

"I want to feel better. I don't want to feel this grief so intensely!"

Julia shakes her head as if trying to dislodge or dismiss something. "Energy is being taken up by the sadness and the grief, by Barbara's loss and all that implies, by all the losses, really."

"And you don't want to feel this grief so intensely!
And you want to feel better.
And energy is being taken up by sadness and grief,
by Barbara's loss, by all the losses.
And when all that,
what would you like to have happen?"

"I have to make a shift and invest energy in happier activities!" Then Julia closes her eyes. Her expression clouds over. "I've been thinking more about that well."

I remain quiet. After two Clean Language sessions, Julia has gotten a feel for how to explore her metaphors. She's already back in touch with them.

"I'm still in it, and there's an antique iron weight, a very large one, on top of me."

"And when a very large antique weight on top of you,
whereabouts on top of you?"

"It's on my chest, my heart. It's on the outside."

"And when it's on the outside,
on your chest, your heart,
then what happens?"

"It covers a big part of me, and it's pressing me down. It's hard to breathe. It's like a paralysis that's not completely unfamiliar, but it's never been this heavy before."

"And what would you like to have happen,
when there's a large antique iron weight on top of you,
there, on your heart?"

"I want to be rescued, to have someone take it off of me!"

*"And what kind of someone could that someone be
who could take it off of you?"*

"A fireman, a rescue person." Julia scrunches her closed eyes. "Now the image of the iron weight is coming into focus: it's a heavy iron black beam like the ones that hold up buildings."

Julia recalls the firemen at the World Trade Center during the 9/11 disaster. "It's like I'm trapped underneath one of those beams."

*"And when you're trapped underneath one of those beams,
what would you like to have happen?"*

"I want to be able to move, to have someone move the beam off. Or maybe lift it up a bit so I can move out from under it."

Now Julia's puzzled. "I sense I have to be the one to lift it up, but I'm under it. I'm stuck, trapped. And I'm unable to see a solution." Even with her eyes closed, it's obvious Julia is thinking, puzzling it out, so I am silent.

"There's no point in using up all the energy I have, all the oxygen, by flailing around, when I need to save it for when I can do something. Right now I need to save it, to lay still and conserve energy and oxygen.

"How much goes on underground in the winter months, we'd never dream," Julia muses. "It is a period of hibernation, a seed-and-life process. It's winter, but things are happening that I don't really know. Eventually I will flower. For now, I can let myself be where I am and stop struggling. And this feels right."

*"And take some time right now to stop struggling,
and to let yourself be where you are."*

But Julia's permission to herself to be where she is doesn't last long.

"I'm impatient! And I fear I'm not doing all I can do. My health is at risk. I can't stretch, I can't move, I can't exercise. It's dark and cramped. I can't believe I should just sit!" Julia keeps her eyes closed, and I sit quietly as she puzzles this out.

She seems to ask herself the by-now-familiar question, 'What would you like to have happen now?'

"I'd like to go to sleep until I'm able to do what I want to do."

Sometimes with new awareness or a new decision, change happens rapidly. Julia sits up a bit straighter. "I'm still in the well, but now I'm able to move around. I don't feel the beam on me like I did. And the garden is way above me, very far up."

"And when the garden is very far up, way above you,
and you don't feel the beam,
and you're in the well, able to move around,
what would you like to have happen now?"

"I'd like to be in the light as much as I can, enjoy what I can of it from down in the well. Catching sunbeams, the warmth. It's the Light of Life, and I need it to live and grow."

"And the Light of Life,
and you need it to live and grow.
And is there anything else about that Light of Life?"

"It's bright, cheerful. There are flowers, colors."

"And is there anything else about those flowers?"

"The flowers are trying to stretch, to reach the light. They want to grow towards the light, through the well… up, up."

"And what kind of Flowers are those Flowers
that are trying to stretch,
that want to grow… up?"

"Maybe a sunflower? No, that's not quite right. A dahlia. No wait, it's a buttercup, a yellow buttercup. It sees the sun, and it knows it needs energy and nutrients to be strong. It's sort of fragile now and needs to be built up a little bit."

I chose carefully which words to include in my repetition and which to leave out, letting the two words "grow" and "up" sit side by side in case, together, they suggest another sort of growing up. But they didn't appear to. Instead, Julia senses this flower knows it needs energy and nutrients; this Buttercup has conscious awareness.

"And when Buttercup is fragile now,
and it knows it needs energy and nutrients to be strong,
and it needs to be built up,
what kind of built up is that built up?"

"It's an inner strength and motivation. It needs a lot of plant food," Julia declares. "It's starving; it's consuming itself. It needs input. It needs help from the outside world."

"And what kind of help from the outside world could that help be?"

"The Light to give nutrients. And it needs water."

"And where could that water come from?"

"There might already be some coming up from underneath. There are puddles, and water is seeping up from the ground. Yes, there's enough. But it'll be a long, slow rise unless the Buttercup can figure out a way to enlist more help from above."

"And if Buttercup can figure out a way to enlist more help,
what kind of help from above could that help be?"

"Someone throws something down—fertilizer. It nurtures. It feeds it what it needs."

"And feeds it what it needs.
And nurture.
And is there anything else about that nurture?"

"It's love, nurturing, genuine care. Someone who really wants to make it grow. It's a cheering section."

"And what kind of cheering section
is that cheering section?"

"It's cheering that knows where the team's starting from and where it has to go. It acknowledges the team is down and encourages it to come back."

"And where is that Cheering Section,
that knows
and acknowledges
and encourages?"

"They're sitting around the top of the well, on the grass. They're having a good time, enjoying themselves. It's a pretty day, and the sun is shining."

"And when a Cheering Section is sitting around the top of the well,
on the grass,
having a good time,
what happens to you in the well?"

"They know I'm in there, in an abstract way, but they aren't aware of me now."

"And when they're not aware of you now,
what would you like to have happen?"

"I need to throw something up to remind them, like a rock."

"And can you throw something up to remind them?"

But Julia is aware of other feelings and ignores the question.

"I'm sitting there thinking: the flower is so low on energy, I shouldn't have to remind them. Are they ever going to remember me? They know I'm there! They encouraged me in the past. They don't realize how deep I am down there. They know in an academic way, but they've not experienced it themselves."

"And when a Cheering Section,
how many could there be in that Cheering Section?"

"I see three to four women now—old, old friends. They're very loving, sensitive women. They're having a picnic. They can acknowledge me, but they can't come down to me. They want me to come up."

"And when they can't come down,
and they want you to come up,
what would you like to have happen?"

"I'd like to come up! I'm the flower, and I want to grow, want the bloom to come up. I'm glad they're there. I'll be up when I can. I want to be there, too." Julia sounds frustrated. "But I don't have enough sunshine, enough plant food."

She opens her eyes. Julia remarks that she takes care of her garden at home only perfunctorily. "It's funny how flowers and gardens keep coming up for me. I'm really not that into them!" And then, without any prompting, she closes her eyes and focuses again on her metaphor garden. "The problem is the gardener of this garden is not doing enough."

"And when the gardener is not doing enough,
what would you like to have happen?"

"I need to find a new gardener, one who is a specialist with this particular plant."

"And is there anything else about a new gardener
who is a specialist with this particular plant?"

"He takes a personal interest in how well the plant is doing. He spends time thinking about how to help it grow and thrive, how it can come up out of the well and into the sunshine. The gardener will have read up on this particular kind of plant and have a strong interest in what's unique about it."

"And what needs to happen to find a Gardener like that?"

"It'll take a little work. And the Gardener needs to learn about this type of flower, what it needs and provide it. And he has to be willing to take the time to read up on it, to buy the nutrients and to put them in the ground."

"And can you find a Gardener like that?"

"Yes. I see him. He's a man with a big, broad hat."

"And is there anything else about that Gardener
with a big, broad hat?"

"The hat is earth-colored, khaki. And he's wearing a light khaki gardener's smock. He's European, old-fashioned. He's wearing garden gloves."

"And is there anything else about a
European, old-fashioned Gardener
wearing a light khaki gardener's smock and garden gloves?"

"He's stocky, and he has big hands, hands that are in the dirt."

"And is there anything else about that Gardener?"

"He's friendly. He's a specialist; he knows exactly what he needs to do. And he takes pride in his work and ability to make these plants grow. He's skilled. He loves the plants. He communicates with them."

"And when Gardener is a specialist
and skilled
and loves plants,
and he communicates with them,
then what happens?"

"He makes me want to come up. And I start to grow because the Gardener cares."

As more details about what Julia subconsciously needs emerge, it seems having someone care is a condition necessary for growth. Evidently it needs to be a different kind of caring than what old, loving friends can provide.

"I grow. And the Gardener is there to bring flowers to health. He cares! And they're all happy in the garden. The Flower is up there with everyone else. The Gardener is the midwife for flowers!"

"And when a Gardener cares,
and the Flower is up there with everyone else,
then what happens?"

"The Flower is blooming. And the garden is suffused with flowers, gold, like the sunshine. The Flower is blooming and healthy and happy, and the sunshine is inside me."

"And when the Flower is blooming
and the garden suffused with flowers
and sunshine is inside you,
what happens to well?"

"The well closes up. It's not a well anymore. It's just grass, and it's a cheerful, colorful day."

"And it's not a well anymore."

I let Julia sit with that awhile before adding,

"And it's grass.
And it's a cheerful, colorful day.
And the sunshine is inside you.
And then what happens?"

"People are enjoying themselves, laughing, having fun. Children are running around. There's a beautiful merry-go-round. Men and women are picnicking. Flowers are blooming, and I'm one of them."

"And you're one of them!
And when you're one of the flowers,
blooming,
what happens to Gardener?"

"The Gardener smiles at me and goes on his way." Julia smiles as she opens her eyes.

The session seems to end with a significant change: Julia is out of the well and in the garden. But as she draws her metaphor map, it turns out that getting out of the well was only temporary.

"It was like a transcendent experience. It didn't last long, but it was a beautiful moment to counter being in the well." She adds an aside, "Drawing is very helpful, recording the images I didn't know were there."

*   *   *   *   *

So, she is back in the well. I resist the temptation to find out how she ended up back there, leaving Julia's mind/body/spirit system to digest what it has experienced. I wonder how helpful this day's exploration has been if she is right back where she started when she came in today. Perhaps the "transcendent experience" will prove to be more important than where she is in her metaphor landscape at the moment. Time will tell. Ultimately, she is in charge of her own healing. I trust in her knowing—a deep, intuitive knowing of what can and needs to happen now, as her system learns from and heals itself.

Discover Yourself with Clean Language

There are a number of symbols in this session whose needs and wants reveal themselves: the Buttercup that knows it needs energy and nutrients, the Cheering Section that wants Julia to come up onto the grass, the Gardener who communicates with flowers and who cares.

If you have two sketches from Chapters One and Two, you likely have several symbols or images on the pages whose needs and wants you can explore.

Not every metaphor you have will be personified with intentions, wants, needs, or emotions. Some are just objects, like the heavy iron weight on Julia's chest. But some objects behave like people: they speak, they may want what you want, or they resist what you desire. Others you may just get a sense from. Just be open to what comes.

You can learn more about your metaphors by taking a bit of time to look again at your drawings and reviewing what you know about each symbol. Ask the Clean Language questions you already know:

"And is there anything else about that [your word(s)]?
"And what kind of [your word(s)] is that [same word(s)]?"

You can also ask:

And what would [symbol] like to have happen?

And is there anything else about that?

Keep asking these questions until you have explored all the symbols on your pages. If you discover new information, go ahead and add that to your drawing or start another.

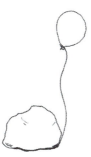

CHAPTER FOUR
A BALLOON TO LEAD ME

Helping professionals, like counselors and coaches, may spend much of their sessions encouraging their clients' explanations of who did or said what to whom and then what happened. You, too, may have given a lot of attention to these parts of your own story.

But with Clean Language sessions, you may have noticed that there isn't a lot of that. Instead, Julia and I are using the time together to explore her inner world, of which she is usually unconscious. One aspect of metaphors that can be hugely revealing and is often out of awareness is locations. Where in the body is that feeling? Where in the space outside the body is that metaphor? And are those feelings and metaphors where she wants and needs them to be?

We all project our inner experiences and knowing into spaces that have some meaningful relationship to our bodies. A significant space might be a particular place inside, like the heart or the gut; it might be nearby in corner of the room; it might be miles or continents or even planets away. As you read this session, take special note of space and locations and how significant they are in regard to what Julia wants to have happen.

Session #4   **September 27**ᵗʰ

Julia announces she experienced an important shift as a result of our last session. She has been considering the purpose of her life, she says, and realizes her self-esteem has come from helping other people as a mother, as a spouse, and in her career as a psychiatric nurse. It was her ego boost, she acknowledges.

"I got a sense of satisfaction putting up with things maybe others wouldn't. Then I woke up with the thought, 'Why are you doing this? Everybody would feel as bad. Why do you have to be the one? Why are you doing that?! You don't have to do this anymore!! You don't have to be unhappy to prove you are a worthwhile person.'

"I realized I've been thinking this since I was a little girl. I asked myself, 'Why don't you do something about it?' With these sessions, I got way far away from myself, like stepping out of myself at a greater distance, in a much more objective way. I thought it was huge!"

Julia has identified a pattern she established as a child—a pattern based on a belief so entrenched that she hasn't been aware of it until now. I direct her attention to shift from examining her past to determining what this new awareness means for the future.

"And 'Why are you doing this?
You don't have to do this anymore!
You don't have to be unhappy to prove you are worthwhile.
Why don't you do something about it?'
And when all that,
what would you like to have happen now?"

"I want to be able to hold onto the insight and run with it! To use it and have it help me with my life."

I guide Julia to connect with this knowing in her body.

"And when hold onto the insight,
where is that hold onto?"

"It's in my lower left side, my heart. It's an inside approach to life. An attitude."

"And attitude, an inside approach to life,
an insight to hold onto and run with,
there, in your heart, on the lower left side.
And you are a worthwhile person.
And when a worthwhile person,
what kind of worthwhile is that worthwhile?"

"It makes me think of my mother and of the nuns and the saints. The image of womanhood. Women who bear all, always good, kind, helping others." Julia shifts in her seat. "But sometimes I'd like to put myself first, not worry about other people. Can I look out for myself, have something I want to do, rather than be looking out for other people?

"I'm afraid of being selfish. I'd like to have an attitude that says, 'Sure, it's alright to do what you want to do, when you want to do it!'"

I want to encourage Julia to explore the consequences of a new attitude that prioritizes her wants. Either they will motivate her to want it all the more, or more problematic issues will be revealed that need to be resolved before she is likely to embrace the new.

"And you're afraid of being selfish.
And 'It's alright to do what you want to do, when you want to do it.'
And when you have an attitude like that,
then what happens?"

"I would be livelier, happier! I do for others, expecting they'll do for me in return, but it doesn't work that way.

"I've made a life on top of a cliff. The canyon and river bed are below. I have a sense that I've built a sense of self, of identity despite that. I do plenty I like to do." Julia puts her hand on her chest as she adds, "But with most important relations, I still have this strain in me that keeps me tethered."

"And when tethered,
that's tethered... like... what?"

"Like a fully formed balloon on a string with a rock on it. I have everything I need to fly and soar, but I have this heavy feeling in my heart. It's a rock."

"And when you have this heavy feeling in your heart, a rock,
and a fully formed balloon on a string,
and everything you need to fly and soar,
what would you like to have happen?"

"I don't want to let the balloon go. I want to take the rock off and hold on to the string. I want to control it."

If Julia is going to figure out to how remove this rock, knowing more about it and the string may provide clues as to how to go about it. Every metaphor landscape has its own logic. Dream logic, I call it, because it doesn't necessarily follow the laws of physics as we know them. A metaphor landscape is more like a dream world where things morph and change and can defy the laws of nature. Still, some qualities about these objects have made them appropriate metaphors for Julia's mind/body's needs, so I guide Julia to take a closer look.

"And what kind of rock is that rock?"

"The rock is big, dark brown, heavy—heavy like lead."

"And what kind of string is that string?"

"The string is fragile, white, a regular piece of string. It's pretty taut, but with a little bounce to it."

"And when a fragile, white, pretty taut string,
where is that string?"

"It's on the ground with the rock on it."

"And a heavy rock, on the string.
And a balloon, fully formed.
And when a balloon,
is there anything else about that fully formed balloon?"

"It's very bright yellow, deep orange, with lots of red."

"And about how big or how small could that balloon be?"

"It's about 1/4 of the size of the rock," Julia calculates.

"And a rock in your heart,
and a balloon 1/4 of the size,
and a fragile, pretty taut string.
And you're tethered.
And you have everything you need to fly and soar.
And then what happens?"

Julia seems startled. "The rock is on the ground, on the string. I can just roll it off!"

"And you can just roll it off!
And will you roll it off now?"

"Yes!"

"And as you roll the rock off the string,
what happens to balloon?"

"I feel light, relieved. I have the balloon. It's not so tightly controlled as it was when it was held by the rock."

"And when you have the balloon,
and it's not so tightly controlled,
then what happens?"

"It can bounce around, feel the breeze, bob."

"And take a bit of time to let that balloon bounce around
and feel the breeze and bob."

"I feel like I want to stay alive, enjoy life, see what happens next, do what I want to do when I want to do it! I can let the balloon lead me around, follow it, see what happens." Julia closes her eyes, smiling. "I see other people with balloons now!"

"And where are those other people with balloons?"

"They're in a park where people are picnicking. It's a scene of happiness and pleasure. I just want to be there, to enjoy being there, talking to other people, watching children, eating, enjoying the sunshine, watching my balloon bob."

I recall Julia's previous metaphor landscape of the garden at the top of the well; this sounds very much like that scene. I ask several questions that invite her to spend some time getting to know this place and experience its pleasures. Then I refer Julia back to a much earlier concern.

"And when a park and people and all that,
what happens to prove you are a worthwhile person?"

"It doesn't seem to matter; it isn't the issue. I'm being myself. I'm just living. It feels so right, I don't worry if I'm worthwhile. This is what being alive is all about. It answers itself." Julia pauses. "It's hard to remember being thirsty when you've had enough. I got my self-esteem from helping other people. I don't need to now."

When Julia has a new feeling, a positive one, I want to help her notice that feeling in her body, to become familiar with it. Reinforcing its presence this way increases the likelihood that she can hold onto that feeling or find it again, if needed.

"And when it feels so right,
where is that feels so right?"

"It's happy inside and all around me."

"And inside and all around.
And when inside,
whereabouts inside?"

Julia smiles. "In my whole chest, my central core, my whole self, and in my muscles."

"And when happy is in your whole self
in your chest

in your central core
and in your muscles,
then what happens?"

"I'm relaxed, peaceful, pleasure-full. It's yellow, glowing, warmth. There's a quiet feeling of fulfillment, joy, and laughter."

"And that's happy inside.
And happy is all around you, too.
And when all around,
whereabouts all around you?"

"It's in the young families in the park. I'm with people, having fun in a relaxed, happy way. It's a Bluegrass Festival. Everybody's giving themselves permission to have a good time."

This last comment gives me pause; I hear the hint of a possible new problem emerging. Maybe it's true for many people worldwide, but certainly in American culture, giving oneself permission to take time off, to be off duty, to just have fun without having to accomplish anything is a challenge for many. Julia may be feeling happy inside and all around her right now, but if she can't give herself permission to have a good time, she may not continue to allow herself fun times.

"And when everybody's giving themselves
permission to have a good time
is there anything else about
giving permission to have a good time?"

"It's harder for me to give myself permission. There's something more important I should be doing than having a good time."

"And when it's harder for you to give yourself permission,
what would you like to have happen?"

"I'd like someone to give me permission."

"And what kind of someone is a someone
who would give you permission?"

"Someone who would say, 'Go! Lighten up! Have fun. You don't have to hold the world up. It's not up to you.'" Julia looks out of the window. "Maybe it's God."

She recalls a statue she has had since she was six. It's of St. Catherine, a nun in a big, white headdress. The memory leads her to recall a very abusive first grade teacher who hit the children and made fun of her. She reminisces about her mother, who didn't have a lot of time for her, what with all her younger siblings.

In some approaches to therapy, a client might be encouraged at a moment like this to explore the history of all this: the teacher, the abuse, the mother, siblings, etc. But with Clean Language, I don't revisit the facts of Julia's past. Again and again I have seen deep healing happen when the client calls upon her conscious and subconscious minds and her body to revisit old experiences and patterns in the language of the subconscious—metaphors. I ask questions that might nudge Julia away from factual memories and into the way she subconsciously applies the lessons she took from them to use now.

"And when a six-year-old,
what could that six-year-old be wearing?"

"A little blue jumper and a white blouse. Her school uniform."

"And a little blue jumper and a white blouse,
her school uniform.
And what would that six-year-old like to have happen?"

"Little Girl wants to get to my mother, to get in her lap, but I've so many younger brothers and sisters. I was always helping her."

You may notice the mixing up of pronouns: Julia refers to the six-year-old as Little Girl, as if the child part is separate from herself, and as I. This is not uncommon, and I find it fascinating to trace pronouns throughout a session. It speaks to the way working with metaphors, including metaphors for oneself, can sometimes offer different perspectives or what Julia described at the beginning of this session as getting "far away from myself."

"And Little Girl wants to get to her mother,

into her lap.
And is there anything else
that Little Girl would like to have happen?"

"She'd like her mother to give permission, to say, "Go play. You don't have to help. Go enjoy yourself. Have fun. Be a kid.""

So, her mother is the someone who needs to give the permission it is hard for Julia to give herself.

"And when Little Girl wants to get in her mother's lap,
and she wants permission,
'Enjoy yourself, have fun, be a kid,'
what would you like to have happen?"

"I'd like to comfort her. She needs help. She's almost beyond knowing how to go out and play. Too much stress. I'd like to say to her that she can be with me. I wouldn't ask anything of her. And when she's ready, we could go and have some fun."

Julia pauses and shakes her head, "But I don't know if I can do that for her."

My next question splits a hair more finely than you might expect. I hear two steps in Julia's want: she has to 'know' and she has 'do.' They suggest a sequence, so I ask about the one that seems to come first.

"And what needs to happen for you to know
if you can do that for her?"

"I have to feel it's appropriate for me to do that. It's too self-indulgent, too self-absorbed. I have to have that attitude inside."

Perhaps it will help Julia to hear her words about that attitude again, to locate it and remember what it feels like—how it felt so right. My review of some of what Julia has said is intended to help her re-experience those moments.

"And an attitude that says, 'Sure, it's alright
to do what you want to do when you want to do it!'
And you can feel like you want to stay alive,

enjoy life,
see what happens next.
And the balloon can bounce around,
feel the breeze and bob.
And you can let the balloon lead you around,
follow it, see what happens.
And happy, there in your central core and in your muscles,
in your whole being.
And when all that,
can you comfort Little Girl?"

"Yes. She's curling up on my lap, and I rock her and she falls asleep. She's relaxing; she's gotten where she wants to be, and she knows she has permission."

"And take all the time you need
to rock Little Girl
and let her sleep.
Relax.
And she's where she wants to be.
And she knows she has permission."

I say all this in a slow, hypnotic way, and then I am quiet. Julia takes perhaps two minutes, eyes closed, her hands at rest in her lap, turned slightly inward as if she is holding something. Finally, she sighs and her shoulders relax a bit. I take this as a cue to continue.

"And when Little Girl is where she wants to be,
curling up on your lap,
and she has permission,
what happens to harder to give yourself permission
to have a good time?"

"It's melting." Julia is quiet a few moments. "It disappears."

"And harder is melting and disappears.
And where is that feeling of permission now?"

"It goes down my throat, through my chest, through my whole body. It's a feeling of normalcy, like, 'Of course you have permission!'"

"And when a feeling of normalcy,

through throat... and chest... and whole body,
and, 'Of course you have permission!',
what happens to, 'You don't have to do this anymore!!
You don't have to be unhappy to prove you are a
worthwhile person?'"

"Then there's a freeing up, and I don't feel as constricted. I feel energy!"

Julia opens her eyes and smiles. She's done for today.

*   *   *   *   *

I'm tempted to ask about energy and what happens now, remembering the lamb and the energy to move forward that Julia wanted a few sessions ago, but a session has to end sometime. I stop here, where Julia stopped, and invite her to draw a metaphor map. It can take the role of extending the session just a bit more. Julia finishes by lovingly drawing a child sleeping in a woman's lap.

Discover Yourself with Clean Language

I introduced this chapter by inviting you to pay attention to where symbols are, both inside and outside Julia's body. Recall the rock in her heart, the approach to life that was in the left lower side of her heart, the happy that was inside in her whole self, central core, and in her muscles (such specificity!) as well as outside all around, where other people were. Julia demonstrates what is true for all of us: locations hold information.

Think about someone or some event from your past. Keep this gentle; choose one that is a pleasant memory. Let's not evoke a painful memory without someone on hand to support you.

Where is that event from the past now? Is it behind you? To the left or the right?
How far in that direction is it?
Or is it inside you somewhere? Where?
Where are you in relation to that past?

Now do a sketch of what you know. Then ask,

Is that past where you would like it to be?
If no, where would you like it to be?

Add any new information to your drawing. Then ask,

And what do you know about that past, there?
And what do you know about you, here, in relation to that
past, there?
And what's between you and that past? And put that down.

Now, ask this next question about details you have noticed. Keep asking the question as long as you keep getting new information.

And is there anything else about that [a word or image from your description]?

When you are ready to finish, ask,

And what do you know now about that event from the past?
And what difference does knowing that make?

You can do this same activity with some event from the future that you want to happen. Where do you sense or envision it? How near or how far is it? Is it where you want it to be? If not, where would you like it to be? Go through the same sequence of questions that you used with the past.

Draw a sketch of your future vision, adding to it as you discover more.

Chapter Five
The Fireman

A Clean Language session gives the gifts of time and patient acceptance that allow deeply hidden information to reveal itself and new coping strategies to emerge. Several times in this next session, Julia wants two things that are mutually exclusive. You might think things are going to come to a grinding halt—that she will be stuck. But people can be open to possibilities when working on the subconscious, metaphoric level in ways they may not be able to be when dealing with the real world, where history and facts seem carved in stone. What is revealed may not resolve her home situation, but Julia finds ways to get hope, support, and purpose. And they come from a surprising source.

Session #5   **October 3rd**

Julia begins today's session describing an online support group she joined. She gets solace from both writing and receiving emails from other parents who have lost children and share her pain.

Then Julia brings out some metaphor maps she has taken it upon herself to make since our last session. "They were a surprise to me,"

Julia notes as she spreads them out on the rug around her. "I never thought in these terms before."

The first is a drawing of a dream. "I felt like I was in a bombed-out building. I couldn't see my way, how to get out. I felt disoriented. You have to feel your way along 'til you see some light and how to get out of the building. I was feeling there was no light."

The second was of what looked like a large elephant and a small person. "Grief is the elephant in the room. I am wary of it. I skirt away from the pain of it, from the pain of death."

In the third drawing, Julia shows herself, a child, sitting on her mother's lap, comforted.

Where to begin with all this? Who better to decide than Julia? I review some of the words she has used to describe each drawing and ask,

"And what are you drawn to now?"

She looks back at the first drawing of the dream. "Thank God they were there."

They? What they? I have no idea who Julia is referring to, but rather than interrupt to ask, I wait to see if their identities will be revealed as Julia continues to talk.

"It was like we were one person, a strength for each other, enabling each other to get through a situation beyond words. The death of a child shakes you to your foundation. It's like the World Trade Center. You go down all those flights of stairs, experiencing everything differently. Your whole life is off-balance. You're off your foundation. The ground has shifted."

"And when your whole life is off-balance,
and you're off your foundation,
and the ground has shifted,
what would you like to have happen?"

"I would like time to reverse itself, to have the buildings come together again, to be humming with activity. The ground solid. Everything familiar around me. I'd know who I am." Julia's slight smile fades completely. "But it can't all go back."

"And when you'd like time to reverse itself,
and when it can't all go back,
what would you like to have happen, then?"

"I'd like to know I'm not alone. And I'd like to get out of the darkness with the sense of destruction all around me, away from the fear that I won't get out."

"And where are you now?"

"I'm in a room with the timbers down and no light. It's a trap. I'm bruised, injured, and I don't know which way to go. I can't see. It's claustrophobic! I hear others crying out, and I want to help them."

"And when you want to help others crying out,
what kind of help is that help?"

"I want to comfort them."

"And you want to comfort them.
And you want to get out.
And what needs to happen so you can comfort the others
and get out?"

"Someone has to burrow in from the top, make a hole, shine a flashlight so I can see the way out."

"And what kind of someone is a someone
who could burrow in from the top
and shine a flashlight
so you can see the way out?"

"A fireman with a yellow slicker and a fireman's hat."

"And is there anything else about that fireman?"

"He's wearing goggles and a mouth protector and gloves. He's calling out, moving large pieces of lumber and strong metal. Other firemen are helping him."

"And as Fireman is calling out
and moving lumber and strong metal,
and other firemen are helping,
what happens to you trapped in a room?"

"I can see a hole of light and a hand with rusty brown gloves reaching in. I reach up and grab onto his hand. I can feel the soft suede of his glove. He calls in, "I'm going to get you out!""

"And as you can see a hole of light
and you can feel the soft suede of his brown gloves,
and Fireman calls, 'I'm going to get you out',
then what happens?"

"I get panicky! I have to let him go so he can keep digging. I'm having a hard time! I'd rather have him down with me. He might go away!"

"And when he might go away
and you'd rather have him with you,
and when he needs to keep digging,
what would you like to have happen?"

"I would like him to give me his flashlight. Then I can see where I am, where the other people are. I could see a little."

"And what does Fireman want to have happen?"

"He wants me to have the flashlight."

"And he wants you to have the flashlight.
And can Fireman give you his flashlight?"

"Yes. Now I'm not so frightened. I can see. I can call the others. I can use the light to comfort the other people. And that gives me the courage to let go of Fireman's hand.

"Fireman tells me he's there; they'll come back. And I can deal with it because I can see. I can see where the dangerous boards with nails are. And the glass. I can help bind the wounds of the others, even though I'm bruised and dazed."

"And as you can see the dangerous boards with nails and glass, and you can help bind the wounds of others, then what happens?"

"I can see the sky. It's blue, and it's a sunny day! Everyone is oriented to helping us. We are the victims. Life is going on up above, geared to helping us get out."

"And when helping you get out, is there anything else about that get out?"

"I realize getting out isn't under my control. I have to wait for them to clear the rubble. I have to depend on others to rescue me, to pull me out. It's very hard not to be panicky."

"And as you wait for them to pull you out, what would you like to have happen?"

"I pass time talking to the other survivors. I'd like to rescue all of them. But I can't. I can give empathy, support. But only the people on top can rescue them."

"And when you can give empathy and support, what kind of empathy and support is that?"

But Julia doesn't answer the question. She's evidently still thinking about the one before.

"What I'd like to do is keep them alive until the rescuers come. But…" Julia shakes her head slightly. "I don't have that kind of control. I can bandage wounds; I can keep spirits up. But they need to keep repeating, 'We will be rescued.' They need to keep feeling the fear and the hurt that is normal to our situation."

"And can they keep repeating, 'We will be rescued.'?"

"Yes."

"And can they feel the fear and hurt that is normal?"

"Yes."

"And as you bandage wounds and keep spirits up,
then what happens?"

"Then there's shouting up above, 'We need to do this, to do that.' There's more help coming. I hear the lumber moving. There's a machine drilling a hole, cutting through the metal and rubble."

"And when a machine is drilling a hole and cutting through,
what kind of machine is that machine?"

"It's very strong! A big, yellow, working machine with a big yellow shovel, scooping up debris."

"And is there anything else about that big yellow working machine
with a big yellow shovel?"

"It's very good at what it does. It lifts heavy, heavy iron and steel bars. It can lift things that men can't. It's burrowing down faster than men can."

"And as a working machine
that's very good at what it does
burrows down,
then what happens?"

"I'm still down there. I'm afraid the machine will make matters worse. If it loosens the debris, it could fall on us."

"And when you're still down there
and afraid the machine will make matters worse,
what would you like to have happen?"

"I wish the Fireman was here with his hand. I wish I could feel the comfort of a human touch."

"And where is Fireman?"

"He's watching the machine work, directing it."

When a person is experiencing something potentially traumatic, in life or in metaphor, one of the things that makes it traumatic is the feeling that one is powerless. My next question not only moves Julia's story along, but puts her in a position of being able to make a choice. It might be about how to feel or about what to do. Whatever the choice concerns, the question offers Julia the possibility of affecting something in order to counteract her helplessness.

"And when you wish he was there, with his hand,
and he's watching and directing the machine,
what would you like to have happen next?"

"I go to the others, and they comfort me."

Did you expect that solution? I admit I didn't. My surprise signals me that I had, just that quickly, come up with other answers in my mind. Without the discipline of Clean Language, I might have suggested that Julia ask the fireman to call down and reassure her again. Or perhaps she could ask to see the light again. Both options are perfectly logical and consistent with her story. But I would have been interfering with her mind/body's learning to help itself. When the comfort Julia wants from the fireman's human hand isn't possible, she finds another way to get the comfort she needs from the others. When I stay *clean*, the power to make a choice remains with her.

"And Fireman is directing the machine,
and the others comfort you.
And when comfort from others,
is there anything else about that comfort?"

"The firemen have sent down water, and everybody feels better. Sandwiches, blankets, band aids—lots of supplies. Somebody's taking care of them—of my needs."

"And is there anything else about your needs?"

"Fireman calls down, 'We're making progress.' I have to let myself let go. Relax."

"And can you let yourself let go, relax,
when Fireman calls down, 'We're making progress.'
and he is taking care of others and of your needs,
and others comfort you?'

"Yes." Julia closes her eyes. In a few moments, her shoulder muscles visibly relax. "I can feel an easing up. I don't have to protect my neck. I can just let it be out there; I don't have to keep it hunched."

"And take some time now to just let it be out there and feel that easing up."

I wait perhaps a minute before I check in.

"And when easing up,
where is that easing up now?"

"It's my whole body." Julia moves her shoulders up and down slightly, and she smiles. "We might as well joke about our situation!"

"And when easing up
and let go and relax,
and it's your whole body,
that's relax... like... what?"

"Like a wonderful warm shower or massage."

"And is there anything else about that warm,
when a warm shower or massage?"

"Actually, it's a hot shower on my shoulders, back, and neck."

As Julia describes this physical sensation that brings ease and relaxation, I hold her attention on it with slow, inviting repetitions.

"And there, on your shoulders... and back... and neck
And as a hot shower
on your shoulders... back... neck,

then what happens?"

"Then I release fear and tension. I'm glad to be alive. Relaxed and warm. I feel safe."

"And relaxed and warm,
your shoulders, back, neck.
And you feel safe.
And when safe,
what kind of safe
is that safe?"

Quite intentionally, I repeat the word 'safe' four times. Just hearing the word again and again is likely to reinforce Julia's experience of that safe feeling.

"I don't have to be ready to fight, to defend myself. I'm being cared for and don't need to be on the alert, ready for the next hit. It's gonna be alright."

"And it's gonna be alright.
And cared for— safe.
Glad to be alive.
And let go,
relaxed and warm.
A hot shower, there, on your shoulders, back, and neck."

As may happen when someone is doing really deep work like this, just when it sounds like Julia has reached a place of healing, she becomes aware of another problem.

"I feel some sadness in my chest and throat."

Before I can ask her a question, Julia demonstrates that her system is getting better at righting itself.

"It's alright. I don't have to tense up. It's a fear of my feeling that's causing all the tension." I wait with her as she sits with her eyes closed. "The fear in my shoulders is gone," she announces. "But my head— there's still intense fear there."

"And the fear in your shoulders is gone.
And take a bit of time to be with your shoulders when the fear is gone."

I gave Julia some time to feel that relief before addressing the fear. Sometimes given a chance, a change in one place or metaphor will affect a change in another. Sometimes it won't. When Julia shifts in her seat, I continue.

"And as the fear in your shoulders is gone,
what happens to head?"

"The fog is still there in my head."

"And whereabouts in your head?"

"It fills my head, like a thick, gray fog."

"And is there anything else about that thick, gray fog?"

"It's damp, clammy, and cool."

"And when a thick, damp, clammy, and cool gray fog fills your head,
what happens when a hot shower?"

"The fog is still there, but I'm more relaxed."

"And when a hot shower and you're more relaxed,
and the fog is still there,
what would you like to have happen?"

"I'd like to release the energy in my head."

"And energy in your head.
And what kind of energy is that energy
that you'd like to release?"

"It's enough energy so I could run ten miles." Without missing a beat, Julia describes the entire route, naming streets and neighborhoods in our city and beyond, a journey that would actually be much further than ten miles.

"I'll run down Charles Street, to the reservoir near Sherwood Gardens, to the Inner Harbor and Canton, around Federal Hill and Fort McHenry. To South Baltimore and the stadium, Washington Village… up, up… to the zoo in Druid Hill Park, to Westminster and York, and back."

"And can you release that energy in your head and run those ten miles?"

"I think so. Yes."

"And take all the time you need to run those ten miles and release that energy."

I sit back quietly while Julia envisions her run. After what seems like a long time, I ask,

"And what's happening now?"

"The fog has cleared up. I know where I am."

Julia opens her eyes and sighs heavily. "I'm sad, and that's alright. It will take time. It's hard to be happy again. This was a true trauma!"

* * * * *

What painstaking work Julia is engaged in. She accepts the slowness of her process, given her loss and the depth of her feelings. She acknowledges her need for help, reassurance, and patience. Her slow and careful pace is matched by a key metaphor in her landscape: the fireman. Just as Julia must patiently work through various aspects of her grief and progressive steps in healing, so the fireman must painstakingly dig through heavy debris to get to her, providing water, supplies, and the occasional encouraging word and touch to sustain her while he works. The metaphor mirrors what is happening in Julia's healing process. It also makes clear that the work is not yet complete.

Discover Yourself with Clean Language

This session was chock full of metaphors that act as resources for Julia, things that help her in a myriad of ways. Think of the firemen, the flashlight, the big yellow machine, and the warm shower. Resources are things that are helpful or that you value.

Looking over the sketches you have made so far, look for a symbol or object you've drawn that acts as a resource. Ask yourself a few times over,

And what kind of [resource] *is that* [resource]*?*

And is there anything else about that [resource]*?*

And where could that [resource] *come from?*

Put down any new details you discover on your page.

Ask yourself a few more questions such as: If you have that resource now, do you have enough of it? Is it strong enough? Is it located where you want it to be? If you don't have that resource now, what needs to happen for you to get what you need?

Put down any new details you discover on your page.

Finally, ask yourself,

And when all that, what do you know now?

And what difference does knowing that make?

CHAPTER SIX
THE DESERT WAKES UP

This next session begins with Julia describing a "heaviness in her chest—a grief." It sounds familiar, like the rock in Session #4, and you may wonder if she has made any progress over her five sessions. But in the course of this next one, it becomes apparent that the source of this heaviness is not Barbara's death; it is a different loss.

Part of what these losses have in common may be the way Julia experiences significant grief. She may have a modus operandi, a pattern of feeling and thinking and behaving that she follows for all similar losses. In turn, the symbols related to one grief may be the same or similar to symbols for other griefs. In this instance, both losses feel like something heavy weighing on the same part of her body.

Clean Language questions help Julia determine how she can alter the metaphors that encode her pattern of grieving. As her metaphors change, whether they emerge into conscious awareness or remain subconscious, her mind/body system will continue to heal the layers of hurt.

Session #6   **March 3rd**

It's been five months since Julia's last session. Family commitments and holidays intervened, she says. Nevertheless, Julia picks up right where she left off, with the same metaphors that ended her last session.

"The fog is gone and my head is clear, but in my chest, there's grief. It's a heaviness."

"And when there's grief and a heaviness,
there, in your chest,
that's a heaviness... like... what?"

"It's a spiky plant."

"And a spiky plant.
And where in your chest
is that spiky plant?"

"In my heart." Julia puts her hand on her chest.

"And when there's a spiky plant there,
in your heart,
what would you like to have happen?"

"I want it to go away."

"And when a spiky plant goes away,
then what happens?"

"Then I'll feel lighter, like a cloud that blows away. A medium-sized, puffy cloud. And the wind could blow, a soft, warm breeze..." Julia pauses in mid-sentence, figuring out how this could work.

"The wind could blow the cloud away if it was light, but this cloud is heavy and painful. It has sharp edges and lightning. Or maybe..." Julia pauses, then returns to her first metaphor. "Or maybe it's a spiky plant—a cactus plant. You can't touch it. So many points of pain."

So, is it a cloud? Or is it a plant? Are they the same things? I'm a bit confused, and that's okay. I just follow Julia's lead and go back to gathering details.

"And is there anything else about that spiky cactus plant?"

"It's in the desert, and it's filled with water."

"And when a spiky cactus plant is in the desert,
and it's filled with water,
what would you like to have happen?"

"I would like to put a needle in it and let it deflate."

"And when you put a needle in it
and when it deflates,
then what happens?"

"Then I'll destroy it. I want to destroy it!!"

"And you want to destroy that cactus plant!
To put a needle in it and let it deflate.
And when a needle, what kind of a needle is that needle
you'd like to put in that spiky plant?"

"A lance. A long lance."

"And where could a long lance like that come from?"

"It's in my hand." Julia holds up her right hand. "It's a gold and silver rod with a silver tip."

"And is there anything else about that gold and silver rod
with a silver tip?"

"It's narrow, like a pole."

"And can you put that narrow gold and silver lance with a silver tip
in that spiky plant, filled with water,
so you can deflate it and destroy it?"

"I'm doing it right now. Now I'm lancing it into a million pieces.

I keep stabbing it as though I'm angry at it. I'm using the pole to knock it over and hit it down."

"And when lancing into a million pieces,
as though you're angry at it,
and knock it over and hit it down,
then what happens?"

"The plant leaks all over the ground, its fluid thicker than water, spreading like sap. The desert is so hot, the ground is soaking it up pretty fast."

"And as the plant is leaking,
its fluid thicker than water,
and ground is soaking it up fast,
where are you?"

"I'm in heavy boots, protected from the plant. I'm grinding it into the ground, grinding until it's all mashed up. The sun is drying the last remnants of the plant." Julia's eyes are closed, and she's making a grinding motion with her hand. "The moist plant is no longer moist. It's green against the brown desert."

"And when the moist plant is no longer moist,
and it's green against the brown desert,
what happens to desert?"

"The desert is quite barren. The plant is an anomaly there, like a growth that doesn't belong there."

"And when a desert is quite barren,
and a plant that doesn't belong,
what would you like to have happen?"

Julia smiles and sighs. "Let it be," she says. "Slowly, it will bloom with flowers, beautiful desert flowers. Cactus flowers with yellow, pink, and white blooms."

"And let it be.
And slowly it will bloom
with cactus flowers—yellow, pink, white."

Then I am quiet, giving Julia time to 'let it be'.

Julia's hand rests in her lap now. "The desert is fallow. The flowers are waiting to bloom, but they aren't there yet." She is quiet again. "They're coming now."

I'm wondering, what might flowers in a barren desert need in order to bloom? And what about that mention earlier about a cloud that Julia could be if the spiky plant was gone? As all these metaphors are part of her internal system, I ask,

"And when spiky plant is in a million pieces,
and green plant is no longer moist,
and the flowers are coming,
is there a relationship between flowers in the desert,
waiting to bloom
and a puffy, medium-sized cloud?"

Julia nods. "There's a fine rain now. It must be coming from the cloud. The desert is being watered from the sky. The soft mist will bring the blooms!" Julia seems surprised and pleased.

"And a fine rain from the cloud.
And the desert is watered from the sky.
And when from the sky,
is there anything else about that sky?"

"It's as though the natural cycle has returned to the desert. The cloud is part of what will make the desert bloom again. A natural event with a good outcome." Julia's hand again goes to her chest. "It feels right, here, inside my chest."

"And whereabouts inside your chest
is that feels right?"

"It's diffused throughout. It's diffused throughout my whole chest and mid-section."

"And what kind of feels right
is that feels right?"

"It's easy and relaxed. It feels like it's the way things are supposed to be. Soon the sun will be there again. Flowers will bloom, part of the natural way. And it won't be so heavy. There's still a melancholia tied to the moment. But there's a natural feel to it now—not angry, trying to destroy. And I can see the sun coming out from behind a cloud."

"And as the sun comes out from behind a cloud,
what happens next?"

"The desert is waking up, beginning to bloom now. There is color and sunshine and blue skies. It's not so hot, so dry, so ominous."

"And is there anything else about that waking up?"

"There's more life. Little animals: jackrabbits, moles, prairie dogs. It's a livelier place now. And coming up from the ground."

"And what kind of coming up from the ground
is that coming up?"

"It's connected to the fluid from the plant that went underground. It was a magic cactus that had to be destroyed and put in the earth."

Here's a twist I didn't expect. Magic?! I think of parallels to ancient Indian and Greek religious stories. How interesting: destruction is necessary for rebirth. This surprise is a good reminder to be on guard about making assumptions about what is good or bad, significant or not. While mashing the cactus into the ground certainly seemed to be satisfying and cathartic for Julia, angry as she was, who knew it was about more than destruction?

Julia and I spend some more time exploring this landscape and getting to know its metaphors. Finally, I review key parts of what she has said and ask,

"And when all that,
is there anything else for today?"

I thought we had reached a place of resolution. But no.

"I'm thinking about my mother, the way she comforted me. Just being around her, I felt everything would be alright. My mother and my father, they're both gone now. But I can still picture them."

"And what kind of picture is that picture?"

"Mother is in a beige skirt and green sweater. She's trim. I notice her lovely blond hair. I'm standing to her left. And on my left is Father, in a lightweight linen sports coat, trousers, and a brimmed hat. They are happy."

"And when Mother is there,
and Father is on your left,
and they are happy,
what would you like to have happen?"

"I would like them to tell me that I was a good mother—that I did everything I could. That once my children were grown, problems or no, I had to go on with my life and let them go. Which my mother did tell me, in fact. As did Dad. He could be somewhat critical, but he loved me. I was always his special child.

"I thought I was grieving for Barbara, but now I think I'm grieving my parents." Julia puts her hand first to her heart and then slides it up to her throat, her eyes tearing, her chin quivering.

"And where is that grieving?"

"I feel it in my throat and my chin." Julia's eyes close. "I have always felt my mother with me, living inside me."

"And when grieving your parents,
and your mother always living inside you,
what would you like to have happen now?"

"I'd like to say to her that I missed her. How much I appreciated her. Still do. Loved her. And still do."

I wait and then ask, gently,

"And is there anything else you'd like to have happen?"

Julia nods and takes a moment before answering. "I need my mother now to reinforce my sense of self-esteem. This last year has knocked me off my feet. Now I'm on my knees."

Julia's first sentence sounds like the way a psychiatric nurse might describe a patient's needs. They are words from the conscious, analytical part of the mind. I focus instead on the words that are metaphoric and embodied—that is, located in the physical self.

"And when you're off your feet
and on your knees now,
what would you like to have happen?"

"I'd like to get up. To focus on things in my life. To feel better about myself. To be looking straight ahead. Right now I'm responding, but not initiating, not planning."

"And can you get up now,
when a mother is always inside you,
and a father loved you?"

"Yes. Yes, I can."

"And take all the time you need now to get up
and find out what happens next."

"It feels so good to stretch and walk! Now I decide when I'm going to go. I start walking, and I'm going somewhere. I'm leaving the house, walking down the road, and just wondering where I'll end up."

Here, the session ends. Julia draws a metaphor map to take with her to help her hold onto her renewed awareness of these resources: her loving mother and father. She carefully folds up her drawing and tucks it into her purse, noting, "This is work!"

Yes, self-exploration takes a lot of concentration and sometimes a lot of emotional energy as well.

"But I feel better. The sadness is still present, but it feels natural now."

* * * * *

It's interesting, isn't it, how exact wording from sessions that took place weeks, even months, ago crops up again in a session? Here it is, eight months after her first session. If you go back and reread the transcript from that day, you will see many of the same words and similar symbolic problems are there. Julia talked about wanting to move forward, needing energy, about being in the desert, watering a green plant, about faraway clouds. But today's metaphors and their details are somewhat different, and Julia is in a different place by the end of the session. The metaphors reflect the change that is happening within.

I recall Session #4, when Julia said, "How much goes on underground in the winter months, we'd never dream. Things are happening that I don't really know. Eventually I will flower." And so it is.

Discover Yourself with Clean Language

You may have noticed, particularly in the last part of this session, how often Julia refers to feelings and her metaphors for them that are located in and around her body. Here is an opportunity for you to experience your own embodied metaphor for a feeling.

In Clean Language sessions, and certainly for our purposes here, we are most interested in exploring the sensations and feelings that you want rather than the ones you don't want. Desirable feelings are another kind of resource, for we can call upon them to help us when a difficult situation arises to which we would like to respond differently.

So, with a blank piece of paper and some markers on hand, ask yourself:

*And what's a feeling you'd like **more** of?*

You might want more calm, more energy, more confidence, or to be more focused. Take a bit of time deciding on one, but know that it doesn't need to be the most significant feeling you want to increase or enhance; just pick one.

And where is that feeling now? On the inside of your body? On the outside? Both?

And whereabouts, there, is that feeling?

Keep asking "whereabouts" until you are as precise as you can be. For example, if you locate a feeling in your heart, whereabouts in your heart? In the chamber on the left? In the middle? In the core of cores? In a room or box?

And is there anything else about that place where that [feeling] *is?*

And is there anything else about that [feeling] *that's there in* [precise location]*?*

And is there anything else about around or beside that [location]*?*

And when you want more of that [feeling]*, how much more do you want?*

And if you had as much of that [feeling] *as you want to have, that would be... like... what?*

Put that down on your paper.

And describe what's in your drawing.

Now, choose any word, image, or part/detail of an image and ask:

And is there anything else about that [selected detail]*?*

And what kind of [selected detail] *is that* [selected detail]*?*

And what do you know about that [feeling]*, now?*

And is there anything else you know now?

By now, you are familiar with this process: keep asking the four questions above as long as you discover new information. When you are ready, you can finish with one last question:

And what difference does knowing all this make?

CHAPTER SEVEN
THE PEASANT GIRL

The reappearance of a problem that had seemed to be resolved in an earlier session does not mean that Clean Language questions aren't helping. When the changes Julia experiences in a session don't stick (such as when she finds herself back in a well or the fog returns), there can be a variety of reasons.

There may be an undiscovered symbol in Julia's metaphor landscape that is calling the shots behind the scenes. We may need to keep exploring the metaphors of her inner experience until the demanding symbol reveals itself. Then Julia can either find a way to convince it to change or she can come up with a way to ignore, exile, or change the symbol herself. Sometimes what seems like a problematic symbol can serve a useful purpose that has yet to be revealed; the system won't discard it because it knows the symbol is a resource. Competing needs will have to be worked out.

And there may be still other unresolved, related issues. Any of these can mean that shifts that happen during sessions may not last.

The good news is that it may not be necessary to negotiate with every problematic symbol nor for every grief to be addressed in order to heal Julia's mind/body system. We are working at the process level. At some point, her system will find a more successful way of managing grief, and this new coping structure will filter back through all her griefs without us having to revisit each one. When that happens, symbols may stop thwarting change without ever having been uncovered. Julia will apply her new modus operandi wherever and whenever it is needed.

In this session, Julia continues revisiting her many metaphors, learning more about their details and working through changes she wants until they are able to maintain a new, comprehensive, stable way of being that serves her better.

Session #7   **March 27ᵗʰ**

Julia arrives looking like what I can only describe as tentative. There's a self-protective quality to the way she arranges her belongings at her feet. She fills me in on what's been happening.

"After my last session, I felt like a normal person. I could just enjoy a beautiful day. I felt clear-headed until the anniversary of Barbara's death." Julia looks down into her lap and shakes her head slightly. "Now there's a fog that won't clear."

I take it as a good sign that Julia was able to be clear-headed for awhile, but then a particularly challenging event occurred, and her system seemed to revert to its old ways—the fog is back. It could be that her new pattern of managing is not yet established enough or strong enough to be able to overcome the emotions connected to the anniversary. Or something else problematic in the metaphor landscape has yet to be uncovered. We shall see.

"And now a fog that won't clear.
And is that the same fog that filled your head or a different fog?"

"I think it's the same one. It's thick and heavy, and there's a numbness—a nothingness. I can't see. It's damp, clammy, cold, and black. I'm groping around." She leans forward slightly, eyes closed. "I hear a voice, a foghorn I go towards, but I don't have a direction of my own."

"And when fog and numbness and foghorn,
and you don't have a direction of your own,
what would you like to have happen?"

"I want to feel clear-headed again."

"And when clear-headed again,
what kind of clear-headed
is that clear-headed?"

"I'll be able to think about the future in more hopeful ways—with optimism and hope. About something other than loss and illness and death."

"And think about the future in more hopeful ways,
with optimism and hope.
And is there anything else you'd like to have happen?"

"I want to be more loving of myself. And I want to be able to look forward to things, find other sources, feel more positive." Julia shakes her head slowly. "I can hardly keep moving. I want to take care of myself and not see everybody else as more important."

"And take care of yourself.
Find other sources
and feel more loving of yourself.
Optimism and hope.
And feel clear-headed again.
And when clear-headed,
what needs to happen to feel clear-headed like that, again?"

But Julia doesn't answer the question. Perhaps she doesn't know yet. Her attention reverts to the problem, so I work from there.

"There's this fog in my head."

"And fog in your head.

And where in your head?"

"Way in the back."

"And in your head,
way in the back.
And is there anything else about that fog, there,
way in the back?"

"There's a buzzing in the front part of my head. And a sense that goes away when I'm asleep and when I first wake up. I'm able to think clearly for a few minutes."

"And what happens just after you first wake up
and before the fog,
when you are able to think clearly?"

"There's not as much anxiety then. Then the fog comes back and the anxiety, and I'm not in control. I'm not able to orient myself in my life because of this fog."

"And what happens after you are able to think clearly and before the fog comes back?"

"Actually, I think that is when the anxiety moves in again. It comes first, and then the fog comes."

"And where is that anxiety?"

"It's in my chest and throat. It's sighing and grief and crying. And things are moving so fast, I can't cope."

"And moving so fast you can't cope.
And when moving that fast,
what would you like to have happen?"

"I would like to let it all out, to break down, express it, get rid of it. I'm carrying around a lot of weight."

"And when carrying around a lot of weight,
that's carrying around that weight... like... what?"

"Like a peasant girl with a yoke and two big, heavy buckets filled with heavy, wet sand. And she can't stand up."

"And when Peasant Girl,
with a yoke and two heavy buckets,
is there anything else about that girl?"

"She's young, 25 or so, and Alsatian. She's wearing a Bavarian festival outfit, a dirndl, with a full skirt in a print over a white slip with puffy sleeves. She has blond hair in pigtails."

"And an Alsatian peasant girl
wearing a dirndl with a full skirt
and a white slip with puffy sleeves, and blond hair in pigtails.
And when two buckets and a yoke,
and heavy... and can't stand up,
what would Peasant Girl like to have happen?"

"I'd like to build more muscle to carry them better. I'm not physically strong," Julia points out.

Here is one of those pronoun shifts again, when she becomes I. Julia is engaged in a dance, at times experiencing this inner part of herself and at other times getting a different perspective on her from a distance.

Julia considers her options. "Or maybe I could put them down and not worry about it. But then who would carry the buckets? I should be able to carry them."

"And how do you know you should be able to carry them?"

"I see others with heavy buckets. I should stop feeling sorry for myself! I'll just keep going back for more, like a robot."

My plan is to just hold Julia's attention here awhile to keep her experiencing what it's like to be this Peasant Girl, carrying others' burdens. Simply having greater awareness and clarity about what she has been doing could motivate Julia—and Peasant Girl—to make different choices.

"And is there anything else about going back for more,
like a robot?"

"She's never questioned if she should carry the yoke. Everyone expects it of her. And she's always tried to do what others want her to do."

"And when she has always tried to do what others want her to do,
what would Peasant Girl like to have happen now?"

"She'd like to tell everybody she's going to have to put the buckets down. They're too heavy for her. Whatever happens happens. This is what she has to do."

"And this is what she has to do.
And whatever happens happens.
The buckets are too heavy for her.
And what needs to happen for Peasant Girl
to tell everybody she's going to have to put the buckets down?"

"She wants to put them down, but they're too heavy. She can't even move to do it." Julia's eyes are closed and her fists are clenched as if around the handles of the buckets. She takes her time. In a voice so soft I can hardly hear her, she almost whispers, "She's afraid."

"And she's afraid.
And she'd like to tell everybody the buckets are too heavy for her,
and she has to put them down.
And she wants to put them down,
and she can't even move to do it.
And when all that,
what needs to happen so she can put those buckets down?"

"Someone can take them off her."

"And someone can take them off her.
And what kind of someone could that someone be,
who could take them off her?"

"I see a couple of strong peasant men. They go to each side of her, and they lift the buckets off."

"And they lift the buckets off."

I pause, giving Julia time to sense the lifting of that weight.

"And then what happens?"

"Peasant Girl falls onto the ground. She's looking stunned, dazed. She sits in the grass." Julia lets out a big breath. "It's such a tremendous relief!"

My next question keeps Julia's attention on that relief. I suspect the expectations of others that she carry the yokes and bear the burden are not likely to just disappear, and she may feel compelled to pick the buckets back up. While that is certainly her choice to make, she has said she doesn't want to. So I focus Julia's attention on her body, on experiencing and appreciating the removal of the weight. The more familiar she becomes with this new feeling and with what happens next, the more likely she is to stand strong under any pressure to go back to her old way of being.

"And when relief,
where is that relief?"

"Her shoulders are starting to get feeling again. They were frozen. It's like she's alive again. They're alive, and there's activity in them. And she has energy now to move around."

I recall early in the session, before Peasant Girl emerged, Julia saying she could hardly keep moving. No wonder, with all that weight! I don't know whether our bodies' symptoms reflect our metaphors or our physical symptoms cause the metaphors to be created. Which is the reflection of the reality? From my facilitator's perspective, it doesn't matter, as working with one will affect the other as parts of a single system.

I repeat her words back so Julia can hear them again.

"And she's alive again!
And shoulders are alive.
They're getting feeling in them.

There's activity and energy to move around.
And when energy to move,
is there anything else about that energy?"

"Now the peasant girl's whole body has energy that flows around. She can stretch and move her neck. She's more active. She can feel herself, her life force."

"And her whole body has energy that flows around!
And she can feel herself.
And her shoulders are alive!
And feel herself and her life force!
And where is that life force?"

"In her back. It needs to stretch, to be a bridge between her shoulders and her legs. She hadn't felt she was alive!"

"And in her back. A bridge between her shoulders and legs.
And is there anywhere else about where energy is now,
when her whole body has energy that flows?"

"Her legs. They're weak; she's been staggering around."

"And when legs are weak,
and she's been staggering around,
what would Peasant Girl like to have happen now?"

"Her legs need to be built up. She needs to start walking around!"

"And can Peasant Girl start walking around,
when her whole body has energy that flows,
and she feels her life force?"

"She's trying to stand up, walking in circles; her legs are still wobbly." Julia's hands have been on her thighs, rubbing them, but she stops, her eyes still closed. "Peasant Girl knows now she can't put the buckets back on. They were crippling her. All her strength has been in her shoulders. Now she has to put it in the rest of her."

"And she can't put the buckets back on.
She knows that now.

The buckets were crippling her.
And she has to put her strength in the rest of her."

I let Julia sit awhile with these thoughts.

"And what needs to happen to put strength in the rest of her?"

"First it has to thaw out. She's still putting a lot of energy into telling other people that she can't pick the buckets up again."

"And is there anything else about those other people?"

"She'd like to tell them to go away."

"And what kind of people are those people
she'd like to tell to go away?"

"Her father. Peasant Girl would like to tell her father that she doesn't have the strength."

A mother and/or father is often the source of powerful 'shoulds.' This is hardly surprising, as we all grow up with such messages.

"And what needs to happen for her to tell her father
that she doesn't have the strength,
when she knows now
she can't put the buckets back on?"

"She tells him, and he's insistent. His face gets red. He's very angry! She wants to please him, to help him."

"And she doesn't have the strength to put the
buckets back on,
and they were crippling her,
and she needs to put her strength in the rest of her.
And when Peasant Girl wants to please her father and help him,
what would you like to have happen?"

"I want to tell Peasant Girl she can't do it alone. She needs to get more help."

*"And when a father gets very angry and face gets red,
what would you like to have happen?"*

"I want to say to the father that in order for Peasant Girl to go on helping him and to stay there with him and to be with him, she needs someone to help her."

"And can you say all that to that father?"

Julia replies in a small voice, dabbing at tears. "No."

"And what needs to happen so you can say, 'She needs help' to that father?"

"I have to have something more definitive in mind than just 'help.'"

*"And what kind of help is that help
the Peasant Girl needs more of?"*

"She needs to get some time off, have some breaks, to rest, to be with friends, relax. She's not built to carry this heavy a load!"

"And is there anything else about that help she needs?"

"She needs encouragement that it's alright."

"And is there anything else about that help she needs?"

"She needs to be able to get away, but feel secure that she's not causing any suffering on the part of her father."

"And is there anything else about that help she needs?"

"No."

Julia now has a complete list of Peasant Girl's needs, but there is another metaphor in this landscape that has wants and needs, too. Being sure this father is heard and that his desires are included in resolving the problems that have emerged are what I described at the start of this chapter as being necessary to assure that, once achieved, changes last.

"And what would an insistent, angry father like to have happen,
when Peasant Girl is carrying two buckets of wet sand,
and she needs some time off, some breaks
to rest, to be with friends,
and she needs encouragement
and she needs to feel secure she's not causing any suffering?"

Julia's next response doesn't answer the question. I recall the previous session, when she said her father was critical, but she knew he loved her. She described herself as her father's special child. What emerges now reflects the complexity of that relationship.

"They're building something, a sand castle," and Julia gestures in front of her. "The sand is there, behind her, and Peasant Girl brings the sand to there, in front. It's a beautiful castle they're building, like the kind you'd see on the beach."

"And is there anything else about that beautiful castle?"

"It's quite elaborate: turrets, moats, spires, walls, doors. Father is enjoying building it. It's pretty close to being complete. We're just putting on the embellishments. He wants to keep building it. He's too old to get the sand, so I am—or Peasant Girl is."

"And Father wants to keep building,
and he's enjoying building it.
And Peasant Girl wants to please him,
and she doesn't have the strength.
She needs breaks and encouragement.
And she needs to feel secure she's not causing any suffering.
And when all that,
what would Peasant Girl like to have happen, now?"

"Peasant Girl would like it to be finished, to sit there and enjoy it. She realizes they have done all this work, and the tide is coming in and will completely wreck it anyway. She's tired of building it."

"And it's pretty close to complete,

and the tide is coming in and will wreck it anyway.
And she would like to be finished
and sit there and enjoy it.
And when sit and enjoy it,
is there anything else about that sit and enjoy it?"

"It's not finished, but maybe that stage is. Maybe there's something else to do with it. The embellishments don't need more sand. Maybe she can sit and enjoy it, and Father can work on the embellishments, reworking it a little better. He doesn't need more sand."

"And what needs to happen
so Peasant Girl can sit and enjoy the beautiful castle,
and Father can work on embellishments?"

Evidently, nothing more is needed because, in this moment, the change happens.

"She sits there with him. He likes to talk to her. To talk about all the building that went into it. She can listen and agree. She can do that with him."

"And Father likes to talk to her
and she can listen and agree,
can do that with him.
And is there anything else that needs to happen
for Peasant Girl to sit and enjoy
and be secure that she's not causing any suffering?"

"It's hard for Peasant Girl to sit there. She's been trying to think that all this work is what's important, when it really isn't. She gets tired of sitting there and sitting there. It's just the same, day after day. Life is over. Just sitting there, talking about the past. She doesn't want to leave him. She'll guard the castle with him, but nothing much can happen! It's nice to focus on other things for awhile."

"And it's hard to sit there,
day after day, talking about the past.
And she doesn't want to leave him.
It's nice to focus on other things.
And when all that,

what would Peasant Girl like to have happen?"

"I don't know." Julia looks up directly at me. She says she is tired and ready to stop. "My throat and chest feel better—not so full."

But before we end, I have one last question to check in with where the session began.

"And when throat and chest feel better, not so full,
what happens to fog in your head?"

"There is less fog. But I don't know what Peasant Girl wants."

* * * * *

Julia began the session lamenting that she has no direction of her own. We might have spent our time together brainstorming options for possible directions, taking into account her interests and skills, hobbies and imagination. But I think that would have been putting the cart before the horse.

Look at all the internal things that had to happen, and still have to happen, before Julia will be ready to take a "direction of her own." Working with her internal metaphors revealed some powerful bonds and 'shoulds'—what she should be able to manage, what she should keep doing, whose needs she should honor, what may be holding her back.

Had I used another counseling or coaching approach, we might have dedicated many sessions to examining Julia's historical father/ daughter relationship. But I have faith in the Clean Language process. This metaphoric father and the other metaphors that emerge encode and embody all the history, the feelings, the beliefs and the strategies Julia has experienced and developed over the years. They contain all she needs to know right now. They will let her know what needs to be addressed without taking sidetracks that may seem important, but are actually unnecessary. The metaphors are Julia's most efficient and effective vehicles of change.

Discover Yourself with Clean Language

Take a look at the metaphor maps you have created so far. Are there problems suggested there? Perhaps you show yourself holding something that you would like, but you don't have yet. Or you show yourself in a place you would like to be, but you aren't there now.

Start two new metaphor maps. Pick a personal issue or topic you would like to know more about and draw a sketch of what it's like for you now. Then make a second sketch of what you would like it to be like and place it beside the first. Then ask yourself,

And what needs to happen for you/it to change from what it's like now to what you would like it to be like?

Just as with Julia, there may be multiple steps involved. Ask yourself Clean Language questions about each step and its specifics to get more details:

And is there anything else that needs to happen?

And is there anything else about that [fill in a word from your description]?

And what kind of [fill in a word] *is that* [same word]?

After all this fact-gathering, you may find that the shift happened for you. If so, great! Just ask the two questions above about what's new now. You may want to draw a new metaphor map or add to the second drawing that you started with.

If the shift you want has not occurred, ask yourself,

And what do I know now about what it's like for me?

And what do I know now about what I'd like it to be like?

And what do I know now about what needs to happen for it to be like what I want it to be like?

And what difference does knowing all this make?

You'll notice that, this time, I changed from writing questions as if they were coming from a facilitator (directed to you), to you asking yourself the questions (using the pronoun I). Which way works better for you? You can adjust the self-discovery questions in the remaining chapters to suit your preference.

Chapter Eight
Tinkerbell's Light

It may take time and numerous questions to uncover the logic of someone's inner landscape. Sometimes she will need to repeatedly collect more information about the parts of her system. What seemed complete or accurate at first may need to get further fleshed out or revised. More resources may need to be brought to light.

Session #8   **April 10th**

Julia settles in her same chair with its familiar view of the garden. The plants in the fish pond have leafed out, and the distant sound of a lawn mower signals spring is here. Julia had generally felt more peaceful and relaxed after the last session, she says, but then her husband had a medical setback over the weekend, and those peaceful feelings shattered.

"What I would like is to get those peaceful, relaxed feelings back."

She mentions the Peasant Girl again and the heavy buckets that were on her shoulders. "The buckets are still there, but they are on the ground now, next to the sand castle. I'm greatly relieved. It's wonderful not to have them."

I'm curious that the buckets are still there. Are they a resource meant to serve some yet-to-be-revealed purpose? Might Julia give in to pressure to pick them up again? Might Peasant Girl? Are they both relieved and ready to move on? This could be a critical choice point, so I spend more time helping Julia locate and notice more about her relieved feelings. Then I ask,

"And the buckets are off
and you are relieved.
And when buckets are still there,
on the ground,
what would you like to have happen?"

"I would like things to stay this way, to try not to carry any burdens. To have what I do in my life flow up from inside out, rather than carrying around the burdens I've felt from heavy sand, from relationships."

"And when flow up from the inside out,
that's flow up... like... what?"

"Like a flowering cherry tree. Or no, like a fountain. Like a beautiful fountain in Rome, natural in the way it flows from the ground up."

"And when it flows up from the inside out,
natural, from the ground up,
where inside is that fountain?"

"It flows from my waist, up from my chest, radiates out from my eyes and ears and mouth. It's a natural energy that's able to flow; it's not blocked."

"And flows from waist, up from chest,
a natural energy that radiates
from mouth and ears and eyes.
And when radiates from eyes,
what kind of energy is that energy from eyes?"

"I'd love to be able to take in what I see and enjoy it, focus on what I want to see, on what is beautiful. To focus my energy on taking it in."

Now I'm a bit confused. The energy was flowing up and radiating out, and now it's focused on taking something in? How could a system work like this? But I don't need to point out what seems to make no sense to me. I just stay curious and direct Julia's attention to details, listening for the logic of the landscape to unfold.

"And what needs to happen for you to focus your energy
on taking in what you want to see,
on what is beautiful?"

"I need to choose to."

"And you need to choose to.
And what happens just before you choose
to focus your energy on taking in what you want to see?"

"I have to make the time." Julia recalls an upcoming Impressionist exhibit she would like to see, with paintings of spring and trees. "The energy from my eyes would pull it in."

"And when energy pulls it in,
then what happens?"

"It would circle in and then back out my chest."

"And that's an energy that radiates out of eyes,
and pulls in what you want to see,
and circles in and back out of chest."

I pause to let Julia imagine experiencing that cycle.

"And there's energy that radiates out from your ears.
And what kind of energy is that energy?"

Julia smiles. "Music!" She mentions symphony tickets and CDs. "I love to listen when it's not blocked. It makes me think of my grandchildren's voices rather than the voices of people complaining of problems."

"And music and grandchildren's voices.
And that's energy radiating out from your ears.
And there's energy radiating out from your mouth.
And is there anything else about that energy from your mouth?"

"When it's allowed to flow, unblocked, there are rainbow colors."

I have not missed the fact that Julia has twice made references to the energy being blocked. But sometimes getting clear on what a person wants is all it takes for the problem to resolve itself. And if it doesn't, she will at least come back to work on the block encouraged and empowered by the vision of what could happen.

"And when there are rainbow colors radiating out of your mouth,
then what happens?"

"That's me being myself. Speaking my mind, saying what I think, not so concerned with everyone else's feelings. I'm content with myself as a tiny force in the Universe, not censored, alright just as I am. Natural!"

"And natural!
And speaking your mind,
content with yourself as a tiny force in the Universe.
And what needs to happen
for you to be "you being yourself" like that?"

"Ah, to stay this way would take an enormous shift on my part," Julia sighs.

"And what kind of shift is that enormous shift?"

"It's a letting go."

"And a letting go... like... what?"

"Like going from a black/gray/white world to a world of color." Julia's shoulders collapse. "The other side of me has a pervading sense of grief, of doom. How hard life is! It focuses on sadness. It's a draining feeling, coming in and pushing me down. It's like a fog, heavy, damp, and black. It's like 'Why bother?' It's taking in the problems, and then my life force is low."

"And when the other side of you focuses on sadness,
and a fog is heavy, damp, and black
and taking in the problems,
and life force is low,
what would you like to have happen?"

"I'd like that life force to become stronger."

"And stronger.
And what needs to happen for that life force to become stronger?"

"I need to give myself permission to do the things I'd like to do."

Permission comes up as a theme again. Evidently, there is yet another layer to resolve.

"And give yourself permission.
And when you give yourself permission
to do the things you'd like to do,
then what happens?"

"Then I'd feel lighter, happier. I'd feel at ease with myself and at peace with who I am. I'd be more centered. Like 'Aha! This is me!' And I'm less resentful of the burdens I have."

"And permission to do the things you'd like to do
and at peace with who you are
and lighter
and more centered.
And when permission,
where is that permission you give yourself?"

"It's in my heart."

"And in your heart.
And whereabouts in your heart?"

"In the top, right part." Julia smiles. "The lighter part of me says, 'It's okay to move on; it's alright to be happy.'"

"And lighter part says, "It's okay to move on.
It's alright to be happy.'
And is there anything else about that lighter part?"

"It brings the beauty and joy in. It's a very small part."

"And a very small part that brings beauty and joy in.
And is there anything else about that very small, lighter part?"

"It's a white light with a little bit of rainbow colors, trying to shine into a darker part of my heart. It's like Tinkerbell's light—bright, circular, like a flashlight beam. Like a firefly."

"And a white light, like Tinkerbell's, like a firefly,
a very small part of that lighter part.
And the lighter part says, 'It's okay to move on;
it's alright to be happy.'
And when a lighter part like that,
in the top right part of your heart,
and when other side is like a fog, damp and heavy,
what would you like to have happen?"

"I would like to spread the lighter side to more of my heart."

"And can you spread the lighter side to more of your heart?"

"The light can't permeate the dark. It's like there's a liner it can't pierce."

"And a liner it can't pierce.
And when a liner,
what kind of liner is that liner?"

"The light can't get through it."

"And a liner the light can't get through.
And you'd like to spread the lighter side to more of your heart.
And what needs to happen for the lighter side

to spread to more of your heart,
when the light can't get through the liner?"

"There needs to be a separation between the parts of the heart so the light could go in the cracks."

I watch Julia's face. With her eyes closed, she appears to be working something out. Her expression shifts with a subtle look of satisfaction. Or perhaps it's relief. I ask,

"And can that light go in the cracks?"

"Yes!"

"And as the light go in the cracks,
then what happens?"

"It's spreading! It's so bright, so hot, it's melting, disintegrating the black material. Once it gets in, it's easily able to destroy the black. It eats up the black from the inside."

"And light is spreading!
And it's easily able to destroy the black!
And as light eats up the black from the inside,
what happens next?"

"It feels good! The vacuum cleaner, the suction is gone. Now there is a pulsing, alive light, like Tinkerbell's, and it's rainbow-colored."

Vacuum cleaner? Suction? Julia mentions these matter-of-factly, like she has known about them, though it's the first I've heard of them. I am again reminded that I will never be privy to all she is experiencing, which is all the more reason to follow her lead.

"And when black is eaten up from the inside,
and there's a pulsing, alive, rainbow-colored light,
what happens to life force?"

"It's going looking for ways to feed itself, for sustenance."

Here's an interesting shift! Life Force now has a need and intention of its own.

*"And what kind of sustenance is that sustenance
Light Force is looking for?"*

"Food, stimulation. But it can't sustain itself without help."

"And what kind of help could that help be?"

"It needs energy to keep the black fog away. It's invisible; it could come back."

*"And it needs energy to keep the black fog away.
And where is that Life Force now?
On the inside?
On the outside?
Both?"*

"It's both inside and outside. I'm more aware now that it's an interactive process that goes on."

"And what kind of interactive is that interactive?"

"It's with the world around me and with my head; it feeds me."

*"And an interactive process that goes on with the world around you
and with your head.
And it feeds you.
And when you're more aware of that interactive process,
where is that aware?"*

"Inside, in my chest."

*"And in your chest.
And whereabouts in your chest?"*

"In my very being. It's a gut-level feeling. But they're cut off from my head. My head has a life of its own."

"And when aware is in your chest,
in your very being,
and it's a gut-level feeling,
and when they're cut off from your head,
and your head has a life of its own,
what would you like to have happen?"

"I would like to not use my head."

Julia rubs her temples; she has a headache now. "The wheels are always turning with 'should.' I can't just let myself be. Life Force wants to say, 'Forget your head and your throat. Let me guide you. Let me feed you with the things that bring you joy.'"

"And what kind of you is the you
that Life Force wants to guide and feed?"

"She's not very strong; she weighs so little compared to her head. She's fragile, with a light-hearted light. And she's waiting—waiting for Head to give its permission. It's a huge head!"

I notice that Julia describes the Head as one that gives permission and, presumably, can withhold it. Logically then, it too has an intention that could be significant.

"And what would Huge Head like to have happen?"

"It's been trying to fix me, but Huge Head would like to rest! It's been bouncing a heavy ball—the 'shoulds.' It would like to stop."

"And when Huge Head would like to rest,
would like to stop bouncing the heavy ball—the 'shoulds',
what would you like to have happen?"

"I'd like to have Head take orders from the Light." Julia puts her hand on her chest. "But there's no connection. There would need to be some connection so the light going into the Head is a part of the whole. All one. The Head part could serve the whole, and Light could soothe the Head with peace and calm." Julia pauses, closing her eyes.

Sometimes just articulating what she needs sets changes in motion. Julia starts talking again.

"And now Head is relaxing into the Light, like it's bathing in the Light. It's letting Light direct its actions: what to look at, what to spend its time on, instead of being so separate."

Julia opens her eyes and looks directly into mine. In a more conversational way, she adds a last, additional remark: "But I don't know if I can hold onto that."

*　*　*　*　*

I could keep going and ask for another metaphor, "And that's hold onto... like... what?" But to both help Julia hold the vision of heart and head and the light as all one and to shift towards ending our session, I suggest she draw a metaphor map.

Putting the metaphors into a physical, visual form involves Julia kinesthetically, using the movement of drawing to bring yet another part of her mind/body into the process of creating a new inner reality. She can take the drawing home to look at again and again and find out more about "hold onto that."

Discover Yourself with Clean Language

In Chapter Five, you did an activity to find out more about one of your own symbols that acts as a resource for you, like Julia's fireman or the digging machine did for her. In Chapter Six, you explored another sort of resource—a feeling you value and want more of.

This time, I invite you to discover something else about your resources: where they come from. It is often a source of even greater power and assistance.

Sometimes resources don't seem to have come from anywhere in particular; they are just there. But sometimes they come from someone, possibly even a divine or spiritual someone or something. Or they come from a place, which could be outside your body, inside, or both. Remember Julia's permission to herself to do the things she would like to do? That resource sense came from a lighter part of herself, tucked up in her heart.

So, take some time to look back over your drawings and look for a symbol that acts as a resource (something that helps you do or have what you want). Refresh your sense of it by reviewing some of the things you learned about it and perhaps discovering something more. When it has "come alive" for you again, ask,

And where could a [symbol] *like that come from?*   (the answer = a)

Repeat this question about your next answer, creating a lineage of the sources of your resource.

And where could that [a] *come from?* (answer = b)

And where could that [b] *come from?* (answer = c)

And where could that [c] *come from?*

And so on.

At any time, you could get more details by asking,

And is there anything else about that [choose a word or phrase]*?*

Eventually, you will come to the end of the lineage. The last answer will not have come from anywhere or anyone else. Then review a key word or two from each of the sources you have uncovered and ask finally,

And what difference does knowing all this make?

Not sure what I mean? Here's an example:

I want a warm light from my heart to radiate out to others.

And where could a warm light that you want to radiate out to others come from?

From a red star. Actually, it's not any particular red star; it's like it's red star energy.

And red star energy.
And where could that red star energy come from?

From Source.

And is there anything else about that Source?

It's oh so loving!

And where could that oh so loving Source come from?

It just is. And it's always there. It always radiates a warm, loving light, and I am always to connected to it, even if I forget about it.

And where could that connect come from?

It's my birthright. I don't have to do anything or be any one thing to be connected.

And birthright.
And always connected.
And oh so loving Source!
And red star energy.
And a warm light that radiates from your heart.
And what difference does knowing all this make?

Play with this 'Where could that come from?' Clean question. The results are often quite surprising.

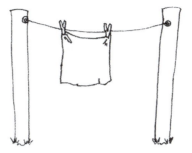

CHAPTER NINE
BLUE FABRIC ON A GRAY CLOTHESLINE

Often as children, with our limited experience and faulty logic, we come to conclusions about our experiences that our adult selves would never make—conclusions we could easily identify now as faulty. We may have reasoned, for example, "If I just never again say how I really feel, I will be safe." Perhaps that tactic was helpful at the time, given the circumstances, but it may have outlived its appropriateness. Now it is damaging or limiting us.

The thing is, we reach these conclusions and adopt these tactics so early in our lives that they often remain below the level of our conscious awareness. We may not even recognize that we have a choice, so automatic has our response become. We may never have questioned or revised these managing strategies from our adult perspective, taking into account our current circumstances and abilities.

Heightening our awareness of the choices we make sometimes reveals that they are based on false assumptions or old, inaccurate beliefs. Realizing this can lead us to set different priorities and make different choices.

Julia comes to this session with new insights into her own patterns of behavior over a lifetime. She has discovered some of her unquestioned beliefs, and she is challenging her old conclusions and strategies.

But the Clean Language process does not settle for insight alone. We will continue to work at the level of metaphor so Julia can integrate these new strategies into her subconscious mind/body system. And if there is still more to be discovered that needs changing, it will show itself.

Session #9   April 17th

It's been a week since Julia's last session, and she reports that she feels anxious much of the time, sometimes for no good reason. Today there are several good reasons, she says, given all that is going on. She spends several minutes talking about what has been happening until she finds a connecting thread.

"It's all of it. It just highlights for me that I can't seem to have a calm, relaxed life, and it's been that way all my life."

"And when anxious,
and sometimes for no good reason,
what would you like to have happen?"

"I would like to be much more laid back, to not let everything get to me so much. My heart, my chest, my throat—they all have one feeling. There's a fearful, nameless dread in my throat and upper chest. A frightened feeling. And my eyes, there's something about them, too, but they are a separate feeling.

"I connect everything," Julia continues. "The day my husband's illness struck was the same day I last saw my close friend before she was witness to a hostage situation."

Julia forged a connection between these two traumas, just as our brains tend to do when our response to one trauma recalls our response to an earlier one. If the feelings are similar, they can become linked. This can be helpful: if we've learned how to cope with an earlier traumatic loss, it can provide helpful lessons on how to manage a new one. But the interconnections can be painfully unhelpful as well, as when, along with a fresh trauma, we again revisit the old pain. We may try to manage it with the same old strategy, even if that one proved to be self-destructive or ineffective.

"It's like I won't get to where I'm supposed to be, like I can't get there."

"And like you can't get there, where you're supposed to be.
And when get to where you're supposed to be,
what kind of supposed to is that supposed to?"

"It's like I'm failing as a person. Everyone else seems to be coping."

"And where is that 'supposed to be'?"

"It's inside, a peaceful place inside."

"And when a peaceful place inside,
whereabouts inside?"

"In the center of me."

"And what kind of peaceful place
is that peaceful place
in the center of you?"

"It's where I'm not disturbed by eternal stresses and pressures, by little things like hostage situations. I should be at the central core." Julia closes her eyes and sits back in her chair. "I long to be relaxed, not tense!"

"And when you're relaxed like you long to be,
that's relaxed... like... what?"

"Like a smooth piece of fabric without a lot of tension, not feeling all wrinkled up."

"And does that smooth piece of fabric have a size or shape?"

"It's about 1/2 foot wide, not large. Well, a little bigger—pillowcase size. It's cotton made very smooth by years of washing."

"And is there anything else about that very smooth cotton fabric?"

"It's light, light blue and it's floating, like a plastic bag in a tree. It's relaxed." Julia exhales softly. "It's a restful image for me."

"And when a light blue, smooth fabric
about 1/2 foot wide and floating,
where is that fabric?"

"It's on a clothesline about 12 feet long, in a large, grassy yard."

"And is there anything else about that clothesline,
in a large, grassy yard?"

"There are gray, metal posts at either end of the gray line. A tiny bit of fabric is held by clothespins that anchors it to the line. It's smooth and relaxed." Julia seems to struggle to make sense of what she sees. "There's something about those clothespins, as though the fabric has some importance. It's trying to figure out its use, and it doesn't want to be lost. That's why the clothespin is on it."

"And where is that Fabric that is trying to figure out its use?
On the inside?
On the outside?
Both?"

"It had been on the inside, but now I'm not so sure. No, now it's on the outside."

"And when it's on the outside,
whereabouts on the outside?"

"Not far. A few feet in front of me."

"And when Fabric is there,
on the outside now, in front,
what would you like to have happen?"

"I want to hold it up to my face, feel the softness, smell the clear scent of it."

"And can you?"

"Yes." Julia tears up. "I'm remembering a bed pillow I keep on our bed—a pretty cream color with lace edges, very silky. My parents had two spreads that my sister made pillows out of. I always remember that spread from my earliest childhood—as young as six years old. I used to love to feel that spread on Mother and Dad's bed."

"And is there anything else about six years old?"

"Huh… yes, there is. That was a bad year for me. I was in first grade. I had a mean teacher who mocked the children, hit them."

"And six years old and first grade.
And a mean teacher.
And what could that six-year-old be wearing?"

"She's in a navy-blue uniform with an insignia on the pocket." Julia closes her eyes. "I remember one time having to stay after school. I was afraid the person who was supposed to pick me up wouldn't wait for me. I ran down to the carpool line, and my ride was the only car left. I was so afraid!"

"And so afraid!
And what would that six-year-old like to have happen?"

"I'd wanted to tell my mother about it, to get in my mother's lap and tell her how frightened I'd been, but there was no room in her lap, what with several younger siblings. I felt like I shouldn't feel that way; I was too old for that!" Julia shook her head, smiling ruefully. "I always felt grown up. I always felt old, never felt like a child."

"And a mother you wanted to tell how frightened you'd been
and a lap you wanted to get into.
And is there anything else about that mother?"

"She is wearing a pretty, simple dress, light brown, with a belt.

She's so soft, very pretty, with long blond hair, curled. She's always well-groomed. And she's busy all the time, always a toddler in her lap."

"And is there anything else about a mother like that?"

"She's always there, but not available."

"And when she's always there
but not available,
what would six-year-old like to have happen?"

"She'd like to make the younger children disappear with a magic wand."

"And what kind of magic wand is that magic wand?"

"It's got ribbons on it and a star on top. It's rainbow-like and sparkly, and it's in her right hand. She can make one wish: that her brothers and sisters disappear!" Julia holds her arm up in front of her, her eyes closed. "There, it's done!"

"And when brothers and sisters disappear,
then what happens?"

"I'm standing there, hoping my mother is not mad at me. It feels like a naughty thing for a six-year-old to do. My mother says, "What have you done?"

"And then what happens?"

"Now the six-year-old is stamping her foot. 'I sent them all back where they came from!' And Mother says, 'Why would you do a thing like that?' And the six-year-old says, 'I need you, too!'"

"And stamping her foot.
And I need you, too!"

"And now the six-year-old is climbing up on Mother's lap, like a baby."

*"And when six-year-old is on Mother's lap, like a baby,
then what happens?"*

"I feel supported and safe, like my mother has lent her strength to my own."

*"And when Mother has lent her strength to your own,
where is that strength?"*

"On the inside, in my chest cavity, a little to the back."

*"And in your chest cavity, a little to the back.
And whereabouts a little to the back?"*

"Now it's in my throat and in my head."

*"And take all the time you need to feel that strength,
lent by that Mother,
in your chest cavity
and throat
and head,
and you feel supported and safe."*

Julia sits with her eyes closed for several whole minutes before speaking again.

"It fills me up with more confidence, helps me feel not so frightened or anxious, not all by myself."

Recall the beginning of this session when Julia described a frightened feeling in her chest and throat? It seems her mind/body wisdom and its metaphors are working on healing them.

*"And when a mother lends strength of her own,
and it fills you up with confidence,
what happens to six-year-old with a mean teacher
who had to stay after school,
who was so afraid?"*

"I'm not so alone in the world. Like someone's backing me up a little bit, someone who will defend me to this teacher. Someone who loves me and cares, who has time for me."

"And when not so alone
and someone backing you up
who defends and loves and cares,
what happens to getting to a peaceful place inside,
where you're supposed to be?"

"Then there's more of the calmness I've been looking for."

"And when calmness
and a mother like that,
is there anything else about that strength of her own?"

"It's a combination of calm, shimmering light blue, a happier shade, and yellow. Like sunshine yellow, more of the warmth of sunshine. It's got a reflective quality, and it's translucent."

"And when a calm, shimmering light blue
and sunshine yellow,
reflective and translucent,
where is all that?"

"It's in my chest cavity."

"And when blue and yellow,
and warmth of sunshine,
in your chest cavity,
then what happens?"

"Then I can take in more warmth of the sun."

"And take all the time you need now to take in more warmth and
sunshine and a calm, shimmering, light blue,
and a Mother who loves you and cares,
who backs you up,
who has time for you.
And when all that,
and as you take in the warmth of that sun,
what happens to six-year-old?"

"She's a lot happier. She loves her mother very much."

"And when a six-year-old is a lot happier,
and she loves her mother very much,
is there anything else that six-year-old would like to have happen?"

"She wants her mother to somehow give her this experience more than once."

"And what kind of experience is that experience
she wants more than once?"

"When she goes to school, she wants to be filled up with Mother's support and calmness and strength."

"And filled up with Mother's support
and calmness and strength.
And is there anything else that six-year-old would like to have happen?"

"Yes. She wants Mother to acknowledge that she wishes she had more time. She would like to have six-year-old on her lap. She would like to take six-year-old back and forth to school, to meet her teacher. She would like to read to six-year-old, to spend an hour or two with her each day."

"And acknowledge she wishes she had more time.
And have six-year-old on her lap,
take her back and forth to school,
meet her teacher,
read to her,
spend an hour or two with her each day.
And is there anything else that six-year-old would like to have happen?"

"She'd like Mother to acknowledge that her six-year-old is scared to death and lonely."

"And acknowledge she's scared to death and lonely.
And acknowledge she wishes she had more time,
spend an hour or two each day with six-year-old.
And can Mother acknowledge all that?"

"Yes, she can. She can remember being that frightened herself. But she had to bury all that. She feels terrible she couldn't be available to her daughter! She did her best. She acknowledges the six-year-old needed that affection."

"And take all the time you need now
to know that Mother can acknowledge all that
and to be with that acknowledge."

Julia sits with her hands cradling her arms, her eyes still shut. I wait several minutes until I see a shift in her breathing.

"And Mother acknowledges all that,
and she remembers being frightened herself,
and she feels terrible she couldn't be available.
She acknowledges six-year-old needed that affection.
And is there anything else that six-year-old
would like to have happen?"

"From now on, six-year-old would like Mother, for ten minutes every day, to take six-year-old in her lap and listen."

"And take six-year-old in her lap every day for ten minutes
and listen.
And can Mother do that?"

"Yes! Yes, she can!"

"And when Mother takes six-year old on her lap for ten minutes
every day
and she listens,
then what happens?"

"Six-year-old feels much better! It's not that she was bad when she felt so frightened. Her feeling of fear is understood, not made light of. It's alright to be six and be afraid."

"And a six-year-old wasn't bad when she felt frightened.
It's alright to be six and be afraid.
And when a mother acknowledges all that,
what difference does that make?"

"Oh, it makes a tremendous difference! There's self-acceptance, self-love, self-regard. The six-year-old is accepted for who she is, what she is, the age she is, even though she has needs and is afraid."

"And what kind of six-year-old is that six-year-old now?"

"She's happier, more eager to give, to be loving to herself, help her mother with the kids. She's not doing it out of duty, but because she likes to, less because it's a should, so she's less guilt-ridden."

"And when she's happier,
more eager to give,
to be loving to herself,
what happens to the peaceful place inside,
that should be the central core?"

"It's right there. The anxiety disappears, and it's a natural, accepting place. I can be doing whatever I want to be doing, and it's alright."

"And when it's a natural, accepting place,
there, in the central core,
what happens to six-year-old then?"

"She's playing happily in the yard with the clothesline material on the line. It's okay to be happy, playing, or frightened. There's an accepting atmosphere where you don't have to be other than yourself. It's a feeling of 'I told my mother my worst secret.' That's over with. I finally told her how I feel. It's a big burden off."

"And when that burden is off,
and you told how you feel,
and a peaceful place is there, inside,
what happens to feeling a failure as a person?"

"There's a feeling of well-being now, like I'm acceptable despite my feelings, instead of continually scolding myself internally. That's different now. There's a more open feeling, less closed, cyclical thinking."

"And when a more open feeling,
that's more open... like... what?"

"Like fresh air, sunshine. More open to experience. I don't have to be so afraid. My feelings can keep changing. It's a less judgmental atmosphere where you have to be careful of what you feel and express. Everything's acceptable now. I can relax."

*　*　*　*　*

Julia said at the beginning of the session that she connects everything. Though her history cannot be rewritten, her internal experience of it can be. When she was able to go back to an early trauma, vividly imagine what it was her six-year-old self needed, and meet those needs by articulating and experiencing what she wanted to have happen, she was able to establish a core place of peace inside and a sense of being acceptable. Time will tell what difference this makes in her life.

The image of the adult self with a younger self on her lap or in his arms, often in a rocking chair, is one I've heard again and again. The person becomes the parent that he or she needed as a child. Sometimes, as in Julia's case, she had a loving mother who was overwhelmed with children to care for. Sometimes the client had a neglectful parent or an abusive one. But what often happens in the metaphor world is that adults find a way to provide their own solace and nurturing. It is beautiful and moving every time it happens.

Discover Yourself with Clean Language

Yet again in this session, Julia connects with a young part of herself. You may be curious to discover if you, too, have one or more inner child parts with some old, unmet need.

I can't simply tell you, "Connect with your inner child." I don't go looking for it (that wouldn't be *clean*), and it usually takes awhile in a session for a child part to emerge and speak for itself. And, in the event that you have some challenging situation your inner child is trying to manage like Julia did, I don't want to take you too deeply into the experience without support. But I do offer you this gentle way of possibly connecting with an inner part of yourself that may be younger.

What I don't do in a session like Julia's last one is assume that encouraging the adult self to comfort and nurture the child self is the appropriate way of healing every inner child. Or that this particular moment is the right time for that. I stay *clean*, and if this is the solution the person wants, then it is right and true. So, if you connect with your own inner child, be sure you are truly and openly listening to him or her, not making assumptions about what he or she wants or needs or about what you should be offering to do. You are unique; honor your own way, in your own good time, of relating with your inner child.

Consider these examples:

I need to push myself to complete [x] *project.*

I want to hold myself accountable.

I need to be more compassionate with myself.

Notice there is an I and a myself. The I part acts in some way towards the myself part. Just this simply, in our everyday conversations, we hint at our awareness of multiple selves.

On a piece of paper, spend five minutes creating phrases like the ones above about yourself.

I want/need to _____ myself (optional to add words after)_____.

It's okay to repeat a phrase as often as you like. Just keep at it for a full five minutes, longer if you like, to let the less obvious ones emerge. When you are done, take a bit of time to read over what you have written. Then select one of your sentences. Take a plain piece of paper and write your sentence across the top.

Now ask yourself:

And what kind of 'I' is that 'I' who wants/needs that?

And how old could that 'I' be?

And is there anything else about that 'I'?

And what kind of 'myself' is that 'myself'?

And how old could that 'myself' be?

And is there anything else about that 'myself'?

Now draw a picture of what the sentence you wrote could look like.

And what do you know now about that 'I'?

And what do you know now about that 'myself'?

*And when I wants/needs to _____ myself _____,
what would that myself like to have happen?*

Add any new information that belongs in your drawing. Keep asking yourself the Clean Language questions you have learned as long as you are getting more information. When you are ready, ask:

And what do you know now about that [select any word]*?*

And is there anything else you know about that?

You can ask these last questions repeatedly about as many words as you like until it feels right to stop. Then ask,

And what do you know now about all that?

And what difference does knowing all this make?

CHAPTER TEN
THE SUBMARINE

In this next session, Julia frequently mentions her family members and 'everyday' reality, rather than her metaphors. It's a delicate dance I lead, giving space for Julia to talk about her external life and have it acknowledged while steering her to her metaphors and her embodied experience of them.

Why not just let or even encourage her to talk about her husband, children, grandchildren, friends, and whatever else is going on? Because most people have done plenty of that before, if not aloud to others, then in their own minds. Given what a fundamentally sound and self-reflective person Julia is, if that was all she needed to let go, grow, and heal, she would likely have been able to do that already. Instead, we spend our Clean Language sessions exploring not the 'everyday,' but the metaphors.

During these sessions, I listen for sequences—'first this happens… and then this… only then can this happen.' I am listening for any sequential steps that Julia takes, checking to be sure that no steps are missing whose absence could be causing problems. With all this information, Julia's mind/body/spirit system will piece together the puzzle of how it works and what changes it needs to make.

Session #10   **April 24ᵗʰ**

Julia is pleased; it's been a really good week. She feels her last session was her greatest breakthrough regarding carrying the fear. "I can still feel it coming up and out. I'm going to keep working on that."

Then Julia begins to recount some of the memories that came up in our last session. She recalls an incident in school when a nun chided her, 'Look at the cry baby.'

"The whole class turned around and looked at me. I remember the shame!" Abruptly, Julia's mood shifts. "I'm feeling so sad all of a sudden."

"And when sad,
where is that sad?"

"It's in my throat and my chest. I feel grief-stricken, heavy, and dragged down."

"And what would you like to have happen,
when you're grief-stricken, heavy, and dragged down?"

"I would like to feel light-hearted."

This is sounding very familiar—a heaviness in her throat and chest. Some element(s) of Julia's system of fear, grief, and shame apparently remain.

"And when light-hearted,
that's light... like... what?"

"It's like a heavy anchor, very large, iron, and black. It holds me down."

Julia ignored my question about what she wants. Her attention is still with the sadness, the heaviness that is so physical for her. I choose to work from where she is in the moment.

"And where is that large anchor?"

"It's deep in the water."

"And is there anything else about that water?"

"It's very heavy, very deep, a large body of water."

"And where is that very heavy, very deep, large body of water?
On the inside?
The outside?
Both?"

"It's inside, in my chest. It fills the whole cavity."

"And when the water is very heavy, very deep, and large,
there, in your chest,
and the very large anchor holds you down,
what would you like to have happen?"

"I would like to cut the line to the anchor and sail away."

"And is there anything else about that sail away?"

"Yes, my husband and I would be on our boat. It would be a beautiful day, the sails would be full, and we'd be on autopilot."

"And what kind of line is that line you'd like to cut,
so you could sail away on your boat,
on autopilot?"

"It's a chain-linked line. It's metal, very strong, and it's attached to the anchor and my boat."

"And is there anything else about that attached?"

"At the top of the chain is a very sturdy nylon rope that attaches the chain to the top of the boat. It's the toughest nylon you can find; it's almost unbreakable."

"And when a chain-linked line
and a tough nylon rope, almost unbreakable,
what needs to happen for you to cut that line?"

"Huh! Did I say it was almost unbreakable? I did, didn't I?" Julia considers two possibilities. "If another large enough boat came between the anchor and my boat with enough speed and with a sharp enough bow, it could sever the chain, could smash through it. Or maybe if the anchor was far enough from the boat, the chain would break."

With her eyes closed, Julia is testing out these options. I remain quiet.

Julia starts again. "Now there's a very fast, white cabin cruiser. There's a man with a captain's hat. He's an idiot. He doesn't know how to operate the cruiser properly."

"And when he doesn't know how to operate the cruiser properly,
can he come with enough speed,
with a sharp enough bow,
to smash through the chain?"

What happens next catches me by surprise: the action really speeds up.

"Yes, he can. He's going very fast, and the chain is blasted in two. It sinks with the anchor. The sailboat jerks forward. And the cabin cruiser keeps going."

"And when chain and anchor sink,
then what happens?"

"It sinks into the silt, even further with the weight of the chain."

"And when the chain is blasted,
and the anchor sinks,
and the sailboat jerks forward,
what happens next?"

"Now the boat is bobbing in the wind. All Alex and I have to do is put the sails up correctly, trim the sails."

"And can you put the sails up correctly and trim them?"

"Yes, nothing holds them back now."

*"And when the anchor and chain sink into the silt,
and sails are up correctly,
and you trim them,
then what happens?"*

"Alex and I sail away. It's a beautiful day! We're going where the wind blows us. Alex is beside himself with joy, thrilled. I'm very happy to be there with him."

"And are you on auto-pilot now?"

"Yes." And then Julia's present-day reality intrudes. "But he's so frail now."

While neither she nor I can change that reality, I can help Julia give voice to her feelings and desires. I ask, gently,

*"And what would you like to have happen,
when Alex is frail now?"*

"I wish Alex was built up enough, well enough, to be sailing on his boat now. Oh, and have our daughter along, to be sure." Julia smiles as she closes her eyes. "The water in my chest is coming up through my eyes now, and it doesn't feel as heavy.

"I feel like I'm grieving my husband. He's declining. I love him as he is; I miss him how he was. If I cried until I didn't need to cry anymore, I'd feel like I could go on with my life, have more energy. I would feel lighter. It's the same as the deep water in my chest and throat. I thought I was grieving Barbara, but that's not..." Her voice fades. She takes a few moments before she speaks again.

"I have to really focus on the losses of, the changes in, these people

133

I have loved. I find I'm able to do it more, maybe half an hour to an hour a day. If I just let myself be, I usually end up crying a little bit, but then, when I get up, I feel much better. I can get stuff done; I can work."

*"And when water comes up through your eyes,
that's come up... like... what?"*

"Like a geyser, a fountain. It's very strong, with a lot of energy behind it."

"And where could that energy come from?"

"From the grief, from the strong emotion, say, if somebody was angry or very, very sad."

"And is there anything else about that geyser, that fountain?"

"It gushes water. Like Yosemite or like the energy behind Niagara Falls, reversed."

"And when there's energy like Yosemite, like Niagara Falls, reversed, what would you like to have happen?"

"I'd really like it all to come up and out. To get all that deep water out, have it pour out. Like the Chesapeake Bay or the Great Lakes."

"And what needs to happen for all that deep water to pour out?"

"The water would need a funnel, a focus to stream up and out. Like a channel or a tube that could suck it in and push it out. It doesn't have one now."

*"And a funnel,... a channel,... a tube to stream up and out.
And does it have a size or shape?"*

"It's a round pipe. And it needs some kind of engine to pull the water in and shoot it out. That's the geyser, the water under pressure. I need to get the water in position to use the energy."

Julia notices something else. "The Bay or Great Lake is empty;

there's nothing there. Everything's stagnant. There's not much life there."

"And when it's empty and not much life there,
what would you like to have happen?"

"I'd like to fill it with clear, sparkling water, like the Caribbean. Have tropical fish, beautiful coral reefs, and beautiful plants. Everybody's floating, snorkeling. Kids are blowing bubbles. Little pleasure boats. It's light-hearted water. It would be the Spirit of Life. The Fountain of Youth. There's lots of color. Lots of growing."

Recalling Julia's first desired outcome at the beginning of the session, I ask,

"And is there a relationship between light-hearted water
and feeling light-hearted?"

"Yes, it's the same."

"And when you'd like to have clear, sparkling, light-hearted water
and Spirit of Life,
the Fountain of Youth and lots of color and growing,
and get all that deep water out,
what needs to happen first?"

"There's an engine with a suction cup that pulls the water in very rapidly. It's green and very big, a strong machine. It builds up the water and shoots it up."

"And where is that engine with a suction cup?"

"It's inside, around my heart. I can see it empty out the lake. Oh, wait, it's outside me now. The pipe is there, just under the water. The machine is floating, like a submarine, right under the water. Now the water flows through the submarine, up and out of the water. It's very strong. The water level goes…" Julia's voice trails off as this continues to unfold in her mind's eye.

I wait a full minute before asking,

"And what's happening now?"

"The machine has sucked the water out. There's a rainbow in the sky, coming from above. All the sparkling water, the coral, the tropical fish are filling up the hole." Julia is smiling now.

"It's like the water has been transformed up in the sky, turning into life-giving, happy water. I'd been stuck with how I would find energy for the geyser, and I found the machine! I feel more light-hearted now."

Julia recalls the vacations the family had in the Caribbean, how much they enjoyed the color, the warm sunshine, the snorkeling, and the pleasure it brought. "The memory of that is so pleasurable, I don't feel so sad."

*   *   *   *   *

As the session ends, something has shifted. For right now, at least, Julia is able to recall a family memory and not be overwhelmed with sadness or grief and loss. With her internal metaphors changed, she is able to enjoy what she had.

Discover Yourself with Clean Language

I started this chapter alerting you to sequences. Julia had one about the sailboat's chain and another about the water shooting up unfold in her session.

It is a bit challenging to guide you through the development of a sequence involving one of your metaphors here, but I can offer you a slightly different kind of experience using Clean Language to learn more about a sequence that is meaningful for you. This will also give you some ideas about other ways you can apply Clean Language, though some metaphors may emerge despite the way we're going to begin.

You'll want to have a blank wall or cleared floor area at least four feet long with as few distractions close by as possible, so remove pictures or avoid patterned rugs, if you can. Get a pad of Post-its notes and a pen or marker.

This time, select something that you "would like to have happen" that is not about an internal change (like wanting to be more confident or focused.) Pick something practical. Maybe you have an area of your house or office you want to de-clutter or a project you want to start or finish. Maybe you want to get around to doing your taxes or stick to an exercise plan. Perhaps you want a promotion and need to brainstorm about ways to go about getting it.

Now on one Post-it we'll call [x], write down a word or short phrase that represents what it is you want (ex. clear desk, write memoir, taxes, daily walk). Place this Post-it on the wall or the floor where it feels right. No need to overthink this; just find a spot.

Now, place yourself where you are in relation to that [x]. You could be side by side or you could be quite a distance apart. You could be facing it or looking away. Settle in and consider your Post-it. Ask,

And is the Post-it in the right space?
And am I in the right space?

If you need to adjust either location, do so and the repeat the question until both feel right. (At any other time in this process, feel free to rearrange your Post-its (there will be more) if you feel the need.)

Now, consider your Post-it [x] again. Ask,

And what do I know from here about that [x]*?*
And is there anything else I know from here about that [x]*?*

And when I am here, and [x] *is there,*
what's one thing that needs to happen before that [x] *can happen?*

And write that down on another Post-it we will call [y], and put that where it feels right. Now stand on [y] or, if you are putting it on a wall, look at that [y]. Ask,

And when [x] *is there... and* [y] *is here,... is there anything that needs to happen before or after* [y]*... and before [x]?*

If yes, write that down on another Post-it we will call [z], and put that where it feels right.

At any time, you could get more specifics about a step by asking,

And is there anything else about that [word or phrase]*?*

Continue on with this pattern, noticing if anything needs to happen between any of the steps you identify. Some things might need to happen simultaneously. Just find the right space for the Post-its.

You may find that some things are happening between steps that are not helpful. If you find one of those, ask,

And what would I like to have happen instead?

Write that down and place it where it feels right.

If you stick with this exploration for at least 10-15 minutes, you are likely to discover things you didn't know you knew.

CHAPTER ELEVEN
THE AIRCRAFT CARRIER

Today, Julia returns to a metaphor that she mentioned briefly as she was drawing a metaphor map at the end of her very first session. She noted then, "I've had an image of myself my whole life as an aircraft carrier. I am both the plane that is caught and the hook that grabs and holds the plane." Now, ten months later, it reappears.

Life-long metaphors are particularly fruitful to explore. If it has been around for decades, surely it is significant. You will notice I ask lots of questions, not just about what Julia wants, but also about what the various symbols in this aircraft carrier metaphor landscape want. If they want what Julia wants, it may help her feel supported and more energetic, confident, and motivated towards the change they all desire. And if they want something that conflicts with what Julia wants? That's a perfect example of an unresolved issue that's been lurking below conscious awareness that I talked about at the start of Chapter Seven. How powerful these metaphors feel to Julia; no wonder her conflicted feelings have been around for so many years.

Session #11   May 1st

Julia begins today's session describing a visit with one of her grandchildren.

"The day was sad and good at the same time. The hugs made me feel such a longing, here, in my chest." Julia puts her hand over her heart and sighs. "It's been a tender day."

"And a tender day
and a longing in your chest.
And what kind of a longing is that longing, there, in your chest?"

"I don't know what it's a longing for."

"And when a longing, there, in your chest,
and you don't know what it's a longing for,
what would you like to have happen?"

"I'd like to return to the days when Barbara was that young. I'd like to have my grandchild with me more, to spend alone time with her."

"And alone time.
And what kind of alone time with her
is that alone time you'd like?"

"I'd give her some of the affection, warmth, love that I feel and that I am not able to display, to give. I'd like to lavish it on her and my other grandchildren. I want to be with them, physically."

"And is there anything else about that affection
that warmth, that love that you feel,
and that want to be with them physically?"

"Yes. I want to receive their love and affection, warmth—that special feeling, so pure, so genuine. To have more uninterrupted time to enjoy the give and take. I want to respond to their lack of guile, to their spontaneity!"

*"And is there a relationship between all that
and the days when Barbara was that young?"*

"They were innocent days, full of hope. We were all going to live forever. It's springtime, the awakening of life. Young lives unfold. It's the fun part of parenting, when the possibilities in front of you are open and endless."

*"And open and endless possibilities.
And springtime.
And is there anything else about that springtime
and the awakening of life?"*

"We're in our yard. I see the swing set and a red wagon. The flowers are blooming. There's a gas grill, lawn chairs, and the apple tree is in blossom. Barbara is in a little coat, a really pretty Scottish plaid coat with a dark green collar. She's in the wagon, waving, and we are pulling her.

"Now I picture her in fall. She is laying in the leaves, and we're taking pictures of her. There are leaves all over her. She's wearing a pale-yellow snowsuit jacket. I'd like to pick her up and hold her and make her safe."

It's not always easy to tell where memory leaves off and the metaphor world begins, but I hear a desired outcome, something Julia wants, and the word safe, and so I engage with this scene as if the people are living metaphors.

"And can you pick her up?"

"Yes, but she gets right off my lap. She was very active. She didn't like to cuddle."

*"And when she didn't like to cuddle,
what would you like to have happen?"*

"I'd like to have Barbara stay in my lap, respond. I'd like her to enjoy it."

"And can she stay in your lap
and respond
and enjoy it now?"

"Yes, and she gives me a hug. She's glad to sit and to be warm."

Recalling Julia's taking her Little Girl self into her own lap (Session #4) and her six-year-old self's desire to be in her mother's lap (Session #9), I linger here.

"And when she stays in your lap,
is there anything else about that lap?"

"It feels so normal! The love you give is coming back; it's interactive. It wasn't normal when Barbara was little, giving and receiving."

"And is there anything else about that feels,
when it feels so normal?"

"It's peaceful."

"And normal.
And peaceful.
And when it's peaceful,
where is that peaceful,
that feels so normal?"

"It spreads throughout my whole body. It's restful. A rose-color feeling. And there are birds. I want to keep this feeling. I could sit like this for hours."

"And take all the time you need to sit like this now."

For several minutes Julia sits motionless. When she begins to stir, I ask,

"And what's happening now?"

"I have a fulfilled feeling that's natural and right. Life and nature expressing itself in the way it's meant to. The way it's supposed to be, but often isn't."

142

"And when a fulfilled feeling,
natural, right,
where is that feeling?"

"It's inside, in my heart, my whole heart. It swells my heart, fills it."

"And when it swells your heart
and fills it,
that's fills... like... what?"

"It's a rubber, bright-red, plastic heart that inflated with air, like a red raft. And it's beating like it's meant to: rising, falling, going in and out, like a living, breathing object. It's so full—so restful."

"And when there's a heart that's rising and falling
and so full, so restful,
in your chest,
what happens to the longing?"

"The longing disappears. Like when I'm with my grandchildren." Julia pauses. "I'd like to have an inflated heart like this one that was portable, a tool I could use to feel better. Like a raft, I could use it to save myself, and it would take away the profound sadness and grief."

"And is there anything else about that raft
that is portable and inflatable?"

"It's a bright-red raft on a dark-blue ocean, an ocean of tears and grief and sadness. I feel like I'm floating. I see Barbara on my lap, a little girl about two years old, but she looks four, in a maroon bathing suit. I'm in a deep-blue suit. I'm keeping her safe. I'm happy, she's happy, we're relaxed."

"And when you're floating on a bright-red raft on a dark-blue ocean,
and you are both relaxed and happy,
and you're keeping her safe,
what happens next?"

"We go swimming, and we're laughing and having fun. And now we're on the beach, the one we took the kids to years ago. We're playing in the surf. And we've got the red raft. There are other families at the beach, too—a timeless scene. How empyreal it all is!"

Julia takes a sharp breath in. "It's really how I want to enjoy the children in my life, but I'm not able to. Alex needs my care now. I want to do both equally, but one has to be paramount."

"And when you want to enjoy the children,
and when you can't because Alex needs your care,
and one has to be paramount,
that's... like... what?"

"It's like I'm in a cage I can't get out of."

"And when you're in a cage you can't get out of,
what would you like to have happen?"

"Actually, it's like this image I've had for years. I'm on a plane, on an aircraft carrier. I'm tethered to the deck with heavy chains. The crew has me tethered. The engine is at full throttle. I want to fly away, and I want to stay on deck."

Here again, Julia has two conflicting desires: to stay on deck and to fly. She wants to care for Alex and to spend time with grandchildren. When there is no solution in sight, I concentrate on gathering more information. Something always happens.

"And when a Crew,
how many Crew could there be?"

"There are four of them dressed in deckhands' uniforms and helmets. They're all men, dark-haired, medium height. They have big signal flags. They are very skilled at what they do, knowing the lives of the pilots depend on them. They have the chains and hooks that keep the planes on the deck."

"And when you are on an aircraft carrier,
on a plane with the engine at full throttle,
and a Crew of four with big signal flags and chains and hooks
who are very skilled at what they do,

and they have you tethered,
what would you like to have happen?"

"I would either like to tell the pilot he can't leave the ship and to turn off the engine or take the hook off and let the plane go. There is an equal energy force in two directions at the same time."

If the symbols in this metaphor landscape have conflicting intentions or options, they could have a part in exerting forces in two directions. They could allow a shift to occur or thwart it. So, I check in with each of the metaphors to see what we are dealing with here.

"And what would Crew like to have happen?"

"Oh, the Crew would like to see the plane take off."

"And what would Pilot like to have happen?"

"The Pilot has been ready to go for a long time."

"And what would Ship like to have happen?"

"It would like the Plane to stay on board where it's safer."

"And what would Plane like to have happen?"

"The Plane wants to stay on the ship. It's a small jet, the kind a fighter pilot might fly."

"And is there anything else about that small jet that a fighter pilot might fly?"

"It's sleek, silver, and strong. It is being pulled in two directions so that vibrations go through the plane and rattle it. The engine is at the point where it should be in the air. It's not really on the ship, it's not really in the air. It's feeling all the vibrations. The Plane would like to give up so it won't be pulled apart. It's in a constant waiting mode, which is extremely frustrating! It's unable to move in any direction. It doesn't want to move in any direction and, at the same time, it wants to!"

145

"And Crew would like to see Plane take off,
and Pilot has been ready to go a long time.
Ship wants Plane to stay on board where it's safer,
and Plane wants to stay on Ship, to give up.
Plane is pulled in two directions,
and it's in a constant waiting mode!

And when Plane is unable to move in any direction,
and it doesn't want to move in any direction,
and it wants to move,
that's... like... what?"

"Like a knot, a very tight knot of the strongest material. Steel. It's impervious to change. It's black, so it is hard to see the knot. It's a conflict."

"And when a very tight, steel, black knot
is impervious to change,
what would you like to have happen?"

"I think the knot could loosen and stop pulling in opposite directions." Julia turns her head, looking back and forth, back and forth.

Gestures like these are more than simply movements; they suggest Julia has psycho-activated the space around her—imbued it with meaning—and it's likely she knows something about what is to each side.

"And when there [gesturing left to where she's looking],
is there anything else about there?"

"To the left are the hooks. They are really strong. There are two big ones on either side of the back of the plane. They're made of heavy braided cable—industrial steel wire. And the plane has loops to put the cable in. They could cut it off, but you would never want to get between them and the plane. They could kill a man if they spun out. They're taut; it's almost like they could wreck the plane."

"And where could hooks like that come from?"

"The four men put them there."

"And when there [gesturing to her right],
is there anything else about there?"

"The ship's pointed right. The plane is on the runway, the size of a football field. And the engine is in full throttle. It would shoot out, like from a bow, up into the air."

*"And when Plane and runway and engine, there,
and four men and big hooks, there,
what would you like to have happen?"*

"I would like the four men to signal the pilot that they're taking the hook off," and she smiles.

"And is there anything else that needs to happen for Plane..."

Julia cuts in. "Now it's taking off! It's soaring into the sky. It's a bright, sunny day with blue skies." Julia adds, "I've never pictured this before."

*"And when Plane is soaring into the sky,
what happens next?"*

"The Pilot is pleased." Julia smiles broadly. "The Plane is strong again. It's able to put all its energy and force into going one direction rather than two. It feels more whole, together, complete."

*"And where is that feel,
when it feels more whole, together, complete?"*

"It's inside and outside, inside in my head, my brain, between the lobes," Julia replies, putting her hand on the top of her head. "It's like I have to hold on to it, thinking about it, because I also have this strong heaviness in my heart. My heart is back on the Ship."

*"And when feels more whole, together, complete,
inside and outside,
and a heaviness in your heart,
and heart is back on Ship,
what would you like to have happen?"*

"There's a sadness about being off the ship, like homesickness. But there's relief and gladness at the total change. A sense of a future and adventure now that I'm off the Ship."

"And relief and gladness at the total change.
A sense of a future and adventure!
And when all that,
and Plane is putting its energy into going in one direction,
and it feels whole, together, and complete,
on the inside and on the outside,
what kind of whole is that whole on the outside?"

"That's enjoying freedom. Flying in the sky, doing loops in the present with no longing. This freedom of not being caught. It feels like an enormous change."

"And doing loops in the sky! Freedom!
And is there anything else about that freedom?"

"I'm picturing the Plane joining other Planes, and they're enjoying each other, not stuck on the ship anymore."

*   *   *   *   *

Julia looks up, smiling. She has popped out of her metaphor world. With a mention of picturing and with our time almost up, I invite Julia to draw a metaphor map now. She takes obvious pleasure in her picture. As she draws, she discovers that the planes are the Blue Angels (the U.S. Navy flight demonstration squad.)

Julia has what feels to her like an 'enormous change,' a new 'freedom' to enjoy becoming more familiar with. We shall see what happens next when, after having had an image of herself her whole life as both the plane and the hook, she no longer feels caught.

Discover Yourself with Clean Language

Do you have a recurrent dream? It is an example of a metaphor(s) that has been with you for many years. If you don't, a regular dream will do.

Write down a brief description of your dream. It doesn't matter if you have variations where the details change or if you just remember a part of the dream. For example, here is how Julia started:

"Actually, it's like this image I've had for years. I'm on a plane, on an aircraft carrier. I'm tethered to the deck with heavy chains. The crew has me tethered. The engine is at full throttle. I want to fly away, and I want to stay on deck."

A few sentences is enough to get started. Now draw a sketch of your description.

Consider both your written words and your drawing, and ask yourself Clean Language questions about both. Begin by getting more details about specific words you have used and about images in your drawing by asking (when x is a specific word or image):

And what kind of [x] *is that* [x]*?*

And is there anything else about that [x]*?*

Once you have some new information, notice if there is anything about the situation in the dream that is problematic, something you don't want. Then ask:

And when [problem]*, what would I like to have happen?*

Get more familiar with what it is you want by asking the same two Clean Language questions you asked about your initial words and drawing of the words. Just learning more about it may be enough to encourage your dream drama to start evolving and changing. Go with it! Add to your drawing, if you like, or start another picture with another "scene."

Is there something about your dream that you want to change, but it hasn't happened? Ask,

And what needs to happen so [the change I want can happen]*?*

You may find your recurrent dream is different in the future!

Chapter Twelve
I am the River and the Stream

Julia experienced what seemed to be some powerful changes, perhaps transformative changes, in last week's session. But as we've seen numerous times before, changes don't always stick. I try to be vigilant about seeing if there is *anything* else that needs to happen to help maintain the shifts, which may or may not appear as the same metaphors or symbols. I am always on the lookout for helpful resources, and in this last session, an old friend returns.

Session #12   **May 8th**

Julia comes in all smiles. She is quick to report that this past week she's been doing things differently.

"Things are looking up. It's been a long time since I felt like this. I'm full of energy!" She's planning a dinner party. She's planting flowers. "It's freeing up a part of me, a subconscious part. In fact, I have so much energy that I don't know what to do with it all!"

Given that Julia talked about not feeling like she had any energy at her first session and that it was one of the first things she said she wanted, and given that she seems so delighted, you might think everything has been taken care of. But I notice the words, "I don't know what to do…" They suggest there might be something more to address.

"And when you have so much energy you don't know
what to do with it,
what would you like to have happen?"

"I have lots more energy than ways to use it. So much is pent up inside me: energy, a longing for normality." Julia says visualizing the imagery from her past Clean Language sessions really helped. "Energy used to hold me down, like that anchor. Now I have cut the anchor, taken a deep breath, and whoosh! The energy has transformed!"

"And cut the anchor!
And woosh!
And energy transformed!
And when all that,
what would you like to have happen now?"

"What I want is a normal expression of energy. I want my energy to flow more evenly, rather than in an explosion of energy. Now there are peaks and valleys of energy, like periods of drought and flood. I want a stream—a steady, continuous source of water."

"And when a stream,
a steady, continuous source of water,
where could a stream like that be?
On the inside?
The outside?
Both?"

"On the outside in front of me." Julia gestures just at her feet.

"And what kind of stream is that stream,
on the outside, in front?"

"It's a peaceful stream that's never lacking in water."

"And a peaceful stream that's never lacking in water.
And where could water come from
that's never lacking?"

Julia points to her left at arm's length. "There's a source that's feeding that stream. It's flowing in a small waterfall and becomes a wider river. The stream is perfectly contained and engineered. Its water is pure and clean, very pretty, simple. And there's a rainbow— prisms of water…" She falls quiet as her eyes close.

"And is there anything else about that flowing water, pure and clean,
in a small waterfall
that becomes a wider river?"

"It's sacred, spiritual."

"And is there anything else about that sacred, spiritual?"

"It's a universal source from which everyone draws. It's life itself. Holy, everlasting, eternal. There's a mythic, spiritual component. It's beautiful!"

"And is there anything else about that wider river?"

"It's calm and blue-gray. I feel connected. My stream is a tributary, and I'm finally re-connected to the river. And the waterfall—it's very important, the focal point."

Any time a person makes a point of saying something is important, it bears more exploration.

"And is there anything else about that small waterfall?"

"I have to be very careful," she says. "I have to be careful to keep it pure, unplugged up, clear of debris that might clog it."

"And what kind of debris is debris that might clog it?"

"Things like leavers and sticks, rocks or mud."

"And when waterfall is pure and unplugged,
then what happens?"

"Then I can keep the stream flowing evenly. It's been dammed, but now the dam is off."

"And what needs to happen for you to keep waterfall pure and unplugged and clear of debris?"

"Someone has to sit there. I have to hire somebody—a watchman. Then I can participate in the stream and enjoy it, rather than be a guard."

"And is there anything else about the watchman you need?"

Julia smiles warmly. "It's the same fellow, the spirit guide, that came before."

I am a bit startled to hear Julia refer to him as a spirit guide, for I've never heard her use that term before, but from her description, I take it this is the Gardener from Session #3.

"He's short and round and wears a wide-brimmed hat and a brown robe with a rope around the middle. He's a peasant. He can watch!"

"And when that Spirit Guide, the peasant, can watch, what happens to debris?"

"He can let me know when I need to clean. He can just check in with me every day, and I can ask."

So, Julia needs to be notified as to when the debris needs clearing. How will Watchman let her know? When every day will this checking in occur? Will she remember to ask? There are evidently things that need to happen to maintain this flowing, and they bear getting specific about. Perhaps there is a sequence of steps that needs to occur.

"And when check in with you every day, what kind of check in is that check in?"

"In the quiet time I take for myself. I just sit and look out the window. That's when I'll be connected to life, rather than stranded, beached. I'll still be connected to the people I've lost. I can take them with me, inside of me. We've all been beached together, flung out of the river, especially Barbara and me. But now we are moving in the stream. She is with me. She loved to swim!"

"And where is this stream now,
when you can take the people you lost with you,
inside of you?"

"The stream is in me now, where I want it to be. There is a fullness now, a contentment. I love the idea of the Watchman and being able to check in!"

"And where is that stream, inside of you?"

"High in my chest, in my throat. The stream fills me up, and I feel less separate, less apart from life. I am full of something other than myself—the life-giving river. My 'I' is like a little wave on a big body of water, and the water is in me, too, inside my chest. In front is the ocean."

Julia calls these biblical thoughts—water, New Testament, fountain of life. "It's very healing to think of myself as part of a whole—connected to those who have died and those not yet born—part of it all."

"And when all that,
what happens to energy you want to flow evenly?"

"I feel reassured. I am filled with an endless source of water. I am part of an ocean or river as much as my little stream. I am the river and the stream. I don't have to do anything. The Watchman is there. My whole body is relaxing. The water flows out to my arms and legs, instead of coming in spurts. I feel calm, steady, even. I don't have to produce. I feel like I am part of Barbara, and she is part of me."

* * * * *

Julia looks up smiling, finished. She makes plans for another session, saying she wants to explore a recurrent dream. Something about the way she talks about it makes it sound like a new topic altogether, and there's a quality of curiosity rather than need in her brief description. My comments in my session notes read, "I sense Julia's need for sessions is coming to an end."

As it turned out, life intervened with Julia's plan for another session. I got a call from her husband, Alex, canceling her next appointment. Julia had a bad cold, and then she was headed off the next week on an extended vacation. She never did reschedule.

Epilogue

As I write this book, it's been more than a decade since Julia's sessions. Once this text was finished, I reached out to her, offering her the opportunity to read the book and asking for her reflections on her Clean Language experience.

Julia brought me up to date on her life. Alex passed away a few years ago, after a long and difficult decline. Julia remains close to her daughter Laura and her grandchildren. She is dating a special man, traveling, and generally engaging in an active life with enthusiasm.

As to how Julia feels about those long-ago sessions as she looks back on them, I'll stay *clean* and let her words speak for her without interpretation or comment.

"I read all twelve sessions and found them very moving. They brought back such vivid memories of my interior life during those dark days following Barbara's death. Some of the images still invoke my emotions, so I know I am still carrying them with me. What I am most struck by is that little bit of light and hope you aided me in accessing proved to be very real and not just imagined and was indeed a harbinger or a bit of my future that eventually blossomed into new life. It was so hard for me to believe that would happen back then, but it did. Holding on to that hope turned out to be the most important factor in my healing. I could not have done that if I did not know it was there! Like all life, mine still has its challenges, but it is also filled today with the color, beauty, and joy I could only imagine back then."

Discover Yourself
with Clean Language

If you have been doing the activities for each of the chapters, you will have a number of drawings or metaphor maps. Spread them out somewhere so you can see them all at once.

Then, take time to look them over.

And what are you drawn to?

And what do you know about that now?

And is there anything else you know about that now?

Continue to ask this third Clean Language question until you find nothing else to know. Then return to the first question and repeat the process with another thing you are drawn to.

Finally, when you have explored your drawings to your satisfaction, ask:

And are there any patterns or repeated themes?

And what do you know now about that pattern or theme?

And what difference does knowing all this make?

More about Clean Language

David Grove's unique way of working with metaphors originated with his work in the 1980s with traumatized clients. His Clean Language methodology evolved in the years that followed due to his innovations and to the contributions of other modelers who have developed Clean processes based on Grove's work. Most notable are Penny Tompkins and James Lawley, whose Symbolic Modeling is the strategic approach I use in these sessions with Julia. Clean Language is used today in many contexts by people around the world: coaching, mediation, education, research, business, acupuncture, and other body and energy practices, as well its original use in psychotherapy.

Clean Language's aim is to foster clarity and change in an efficient, effective, and deeply respectful way. It optimizes the conditions necessary for people to discover information from their conscious mind, subconscious mind, and physical and energetic body.

Clean Language questions can be used for any sort of information gathering. The topic might be practical: making a plan for launching a new business, determining a process for identifying the best candidate for a new job position, or clarifying someone's leadership style. Or it can be used to generate ideas for a book or song or work of art. Any complex or creative process can be made clearer with Clean Language.

Clean Language can also help people communicate better with one another. When you are clearer about what you mean and what you want and clearer about what other people mean and what they want, resolving conflicts and working together get much easier.

As you have witnessed in this book, Clean Language is also extraordinarily effective at accessing the metaphors that reveal a person's inner world, a place of wisdom and confusions, of strengths and weaknesses, of fears and desires, of life-long patterns and stubborn blocks. Changes at this level can bring about not just adjustments, but transformation.

What's *clean* about Clean Language?

If I was talking with Julia in a normal social context, I would most likely listen for opportunities to match my experience with hers, to find common ground and share my stories as a way of building our connection and friendship. In a therapeutic context, depending on my methodology, I might encourage Julia to take what I believe would be a more helpful perspective. Or I might suggest actions or activities designed to help her find her own way to that perspective.

In conducting a Clean Language session, however, I meet Julia with a different intention. The term *clean* refers to the goal of not adding to nor changing the person's content. I seek to stay *clean* by keeping my agenda, insights, interpretations, and advice from "contaminating" Julia's exploratory experience. I can't avoid having these thoughts, but I keep them to myself. I even take care to refrain from inserting my own metaphors, the ones that lace my speech without my noticing it, for they could lead the client. (Words like inserting, lace, and lead in that last sentence are all suggestive of metaphors.) I avoid inserting my own "stuff" by asking very simple questions, carefully devised and tested by David Grove, about Julia's exact words. I add no other words of my own. Rather than altering the content of her sessions, I direct Julia's attention to selected words, phrases, symbols, and metaphors that are entirely her own. Yes, there is a strategy to my choices of which of her words to ask about, but I stay *clean*.

Thus, I listen in a unique way. I am not running Julia's words and experiences through my own history of experiences, my other clients' experiences, or what I may have read from theorists. In the moment, I am fully concentrating on what she says she wants to happen and the metaphors that emerge for her, trusting she has the wisdom within to know what to do about them. Staying *clean* means I allow her to be with her own words, thoughts, emotions, and memories—to really be with them.

Be a fly on the wall to any conversation you witness on TV or between people in your presence. Notice how we only give one another the opportunity to be with our words for very short periods of time. And that may be entirely reasonable for many conversations.

But when someone wants to get clarity on something they are struggling with, time spent exploring themselves without distraction or interruption can be a great gift. People are far more capable of achieving profound insights, shifts, healing, and growth than we often give them credit for. What they need is quiet time, listening, directed attention, and an awareness of their internal metaphors.

Where to learn more

You can learn more about Clean Language on my website, **www.cleanlanguageresources.com.** I've written several books on the subject, listed below. I use them as the texts for my training courses, but individuals wanting to learn to conduct sessions themselves find the workbooks useful as introductions to Clean Language and as self-training tools. I encourage people interested in learning to facilitate using Clean Language to have a session themselves first. I offer them over the Internet to people curious about training. If you are simply interested in your own growth, I also offer online sessions for people seeking personal development.

Panning for Your Client's Gold: 12 Lean Clean Language Processes (2015) by Gina Campbell. These Clean processes, developed by David Grove in his later years, use Clean Language questions to explore what clients can learn from moving in space and from working with their own stick-figure drawings where their metaphors can readily been seen and remembered. Easier to learn than Clean Language because they are script-based, these processes can be powerful agents of clarity and change, too. One-on-one and group processes are included.

Mining Your Client's Metaphors: A How-To Workbook on Clean Language and Symbolic Modeling, Basics Part One: Facilitating Clarity (2012) by Gina Campbell. The title says it all. This is step-by-step workbook, structured with explanations, examples, and activities to learn and practice 9 basic Clean Language questions and the same Symbolic Modeling strategies employed in Julia's sessions to help people learn more about themselves.

Mining Your Client's Metaphors: A How-To Workbook on Clean Language and Symbolic Modeling, Basics Part Two: Facilitating Change (2013) by Gina Campbell. This workbook takes the Clean Language questions from Part One to a deeper level and adds new questions and strategies to work with clients who want changes that did not happen with greater clarity alone. Julia's sessions employed these skills, too.

A tremendously rich resource for all things Clean is the website **www.cleanlanguage.co.uk.** With over 200 articles, many by James Lawley and Penny Tompkins, the pre-eminent leaders in the field, you will find endless Clean tributaries to meander down.

Other books focused on the sort of Clean Language sessions I do with Julia include:

Metaphors in Mind: Transformation through Symbolic Modelling (2000) by James Lawley and Penny Tompkins.

Trust Me, I'm the Patient: Clean Language, Metaphor, and the New Psychology of Change (2012) by Philip Harland.

Words that Touch: How to Ask Questions Your Body Can Answer (12 Essential "Clean Questions" for Mind/Body Therapists) (2017) by Nick Pole.

Clean Language: Revealing Metaphors and Opening Minds (2008) by Wendy Sullivan and Judy Rees.

Clean Approaches for Coaches: Create the Conditions for Change Using Clean Language and Symbolic Modelling (2013) by Marian Way.

ACKNOWLEDGMENTS

First, I must thank Julia, who gave me permission to use her sessions. In keeping with her life-long devotion to helping others, she has again made a significant contribution by helping enhance awareness of this powerful healing tool, Clean Language.

I want to acknowledge the genius of David Grove, who first developed Clean Language. The longer I use Clean processes with clients, the more my appreciation grows for what seems simple, but is actually profoundly insightful and subtle. Equally as significant for me are the contributions Penny Tompkins and James Lawley, developers of Symbolic Modeling, have made to the field. My thanks to them both for their continued teaching, mentoring, insight, and abiding friendship.

Having readers who offer constructive feedback is always helpful, and this book evolved significantly in response to suggestions offered by Susan Fleishman, Peggy Heller, Chaddie Hughes, Germaine Lanaux, Jill Rowan, and Ricardo Sierra. Thank you!

About the Author

 After many years of teaching both children and adults, Gina Campbell switched gears to pursue a Master's degree in School Counseling. Though she completed her mental health degree, she never became a school counselor because she was bitten by the Clean Language bug. A devotee ever since, she applies her decades of teaching and developmental counseling experience to impart the basic skills and the nuances of Clean Language to intrigued helping and healing professionals through her writing and trainings. A Certified Clean Language Practitioner (CCP), as well as a Certified Applied Poetry Facilitator (CAPF) through the International Federation for Biblio/Poetry Therapy, she is an expert in the use of metaphor to help clients grow and change. She lives in Baltimore, Maryland (USA).

Printed in the United States
by Baker & Taylor Publisher Services